People Driven Leadership

How the Best 9-1-1 Centers Inspire Positive Change

Adam Timm

Printed in the United states of America
ISBN 13: 978-0-578-66641-9

www.thehealthydispatcher.com

To my wife

/

To the everyday superheroes—
The men & women working in emergency
communications centers across the country

TABLE OF CONTENTS

Acknowledgments **1**

Introduction **3**

PART ONE: BEING THE TYPE OF LEADER THE CENTER NEEDS **9**

Chapter 1: Where Are All The People Driven Leaders? 11

Chapter 2: Not a Technical "Staffing" Issue but an Adaptive "People" Issue 17

Which Practices Are Most Effective? 18

An Adaptive Fix to a Technical Challenge 25

Chapter 3: People Driven Leadership is the Key to an Adaptive Approach 29

Know Thyself and Others: The Power of Emotional Intelligence 30

From Emotional Intelligence Flows Values 35

From Values Flows Expectations 40

Commitment to Finding the Best Way: Excellence 42

Creating Ownership and Buy-In: Inspiring Trust 46

The Five Key Characteristics of a People Driven Leader 52

Chapter 4: Being the Type of Leader You'd Want to Follow 55

People Driven Leader Profile 57

What the 9-1-1 Industry Says About People Driven Leadership 61

The Signs of a People Driven Center 63

Chapter 5: Culture and Climate: How and Why the Soft Stuff Matters 71

Climate 72

Culture Eats Strategy for Breakfast 74

Chapter 6: Assessing Whether Your Center is People Oriented 77

PART TWO: TRANSFORMATION **81**

Chapter 7: Vision: We're Lost Without It 83

Stepping Forward 85

The Process of Understanding Your Center's Vision 87

Summary: Bringing the Vision to Your Team 95

Chapter 8: Trust is More Than a Feeling 99

Turning Vision into Results 99

Putting First Things First 102

A Certain Kind of Trust 103

Chapter 9: A Better Way to Communicate 109

The Emotionally Intelligent Communicator 111

Chapter 10: Integrity in Action 117
Chapter 11: The Art of Managing Transitions 123
Mismanaged Transition 125
The Most Important Steps 125
Give Them Something to Own 128
Quantify the Intangibles 128
Ask for Feedback — Talk to Your People! 130
Turn to the Metrics 132
Chapter 12: Make Your Culture Work For You 137
The Change Agents 145
Chapter 13: Without Accountability, There is No Standard 149
Working with Violated Expectations 151
No Accountability, No Team 153
PART THREE: SUSTAINING THE CHANGE 157
Chapter 14: Getting the Right People in the Seats 159
Recruiting and Hiring the Right People 159
Chapter 15: Manage Performance with Feedback 167
The Power of a QA Approach 170
Chapter 16: If You Don't Coach Them, They Won't Learn 175
The GROW Model 176
Chapter 17: The Power of Employee Engagement 183
Appreciation, Recognition & Motivation 186
Herzberg's Two-Factor Theory 190
Chapter 18: Training and Development 195
The Importance of Conferences 198
Advancement Opportunity 199
Chapter 19: Prioritize Employee Health 201
Bring Expectations in Line with Reality 206
The Expendables 207
Prioritizing Your People is about Risk and Liability 210
Low Staffing Prevents Proactive Measures 211
Chapter 20: Dare to Tell a New Story 215
The High Performing PSAP 217
What is the Opportunity? 219
Suggestions for Further Reading 221
About the Author 224

ACKNOWLEDGMENTS

I'm continually amazed by the efforts of the 9-1-1 professionals I meet across the country. You sacrifice so much for the communities you serve. Thank you for allowing me the opportunity to serve you.

I couldn't write this book without learning from some of the most dedicated, purpose-driven and humble People Driven Leaders in the country. It's an honor to be able to share your stories.

Melissa Alterio, thank you for your daring and vulnerability. **Becky Bacon**, thank you for your dedication to helping your people find their best way. **Lynn Bowler**, thank you for your love and devotion to the industry; you are a legend. **Chad Chewning**, thank you for clearly demonstrating the power of vision; and **Joni Harvey**, **Erica Cook**, thank you for sharing the challenges you've overcome. **Chief Conger**, thank you for setting a standard we all can follow. **LaDonna Coriell**, thank you for giving your people hope and faith again. **Nick DiCicco** and **Lisa Davet**, thank you for sharing your family values; and **Nancy Lohnes Jewitt**, **Christine Mayzzeo**, **Karen Cassese**, **Justin Kyreme-Parks**, thank you for helping me experience the feeling of working at such a great center. **Ron Dunn**, thank you for your innovative approach. **Chris Freeman**, thank you for always believing in a better way. **Mary Garrett**, thank you for your unwavering tenacity. **Tom Holman,** thank you for breaking the old mold. **Don Jones**, thank you for you being the type of leader I would love to work for. **Joel Justice**, thank you for having the courage to take on a huge goal without knowing where it might lead. **Carolyn Lewis**, thank you for being the voice for your people when they didn't feel heard. **Rosanna McKinney**, thank you for continuing your work. **Monica Million**, thank you for letting your values lead the way. **Captain**

Leonard Montgomery, thank you for creating an environment where motivation is inevitable; **Bud Gray**, thank you for making life easier for those under your charge; and **Antigudra Clayton**, thank you for sharing your story. **Melanie Neal**, thank you for always taking the high road. **Shannon Price**, thank you for making yours a center to be proud of; and **Stephanie Galvan**, thank you for committing to rise above the crustiness. **Carl Simpson**, thank you for seeing the ship through your crew's eyes. **Carl Stephens**, thank you for creating cheerleaders. **Ivan Whitaker**, thank you for trusting your people could and would own it.

Thank you to the People Driven Leaders at emergency communications centers across the country I haven't yet met. Your efforts are changing the industry and improving lives, one center at a time.

You've each shown us what's possible. Thank you.

INTRODUCTION

If you've managed or supervised a 9-1-1 communications center, you're familiar with the commonality of the industry's perennial problems. High turnover. Low morale. Caustic negativity. Excessive sick time usage. Mandatory overtime. The problems have become so commonplace, you could call them "business as usual." More than one communications center director has said to a local news outlet, when commenting on the staffing challenges at their center, "This isn't just a local problem; it's a national problem."

This book will not focus on these problems. There has been much thought and discussion, rightfully so, focused on what is wrong in the 9-1-1 industry.

Instead, this book draws on in-depth research conducted at more than two dozen 9-1-1 communications centers across the country that have successfully changed the culture of their centers. These centers have reduced sick time usage by over 50%, halved spending on OT, and improved trainee success rates by 60%. They have gone from an average of 40% turnover to virtually eliminating turnover.

While doing this research, I discovered something surprising. As complicated and overwhelming as these issues may seem, the solution was deceptively simple. All the high-performing centers I worked with had one element in common: what I call "People Driven Leaders."

People Driven Leaders had dramatically reduced sick time usage, halved spending on OT, and improved trainee success rates by leaps and bounds. In short, they had turned their centers into places where people wanted to work. The good news is that anyone can become a People Driven Leader if they take the initiative to understand how.

By delving into the important work done at their centers and the model created by these People Driven Leaders, I have created a blueprint for you to create your own People Driven Center.

HOW TO USE THIS BOOK

In these pages, the seeming mystery around successful comm center change initiatives is made clear and accessible. "How did they do that?" we might ask, as we then say, "I sure wish we could, too." This book shows that there are consistent practices leaders can use to evaluate, diagnose, and then change their organizations for the better. There is no mystery, and these successes can be duplicated. With these step-by-step strategies, you can address and overcome the most pressing challenges your center faces today.

This book is divided into three parts. Applying each one will allow you to boost employee morale and inspire high performance culture at your center.

Part One lays out the vital foundation for change: the characteristics of a People Driven Leader. The chapters in this section explain first why a different type of leader is required to solve the challenges faced by the 9-1-1 industry. You will learn the signs to look for and how to assess whether your center is People Driven.

Part Two offers insights on how to successfully manage the transformation into a People Driven Center. We'll begin with how to create a compelling leadership vision—one that motivates and inspires. You'll learn the following: how to turn this vision into results, a better way to communicate, and the importance of integrity and accountability.

Part Three shows you how to sustain the momentum of this transformation. The most amazing changes will not stick if you don't plan for succession. The chapters in this section share how to work with your team in the most effective way possible, using coaching and regular feedback. We'll discuss employee engagement, training and development, and the profound impact of prioritizing employee health. Finally, you'll be invited to tell a new story about your center.

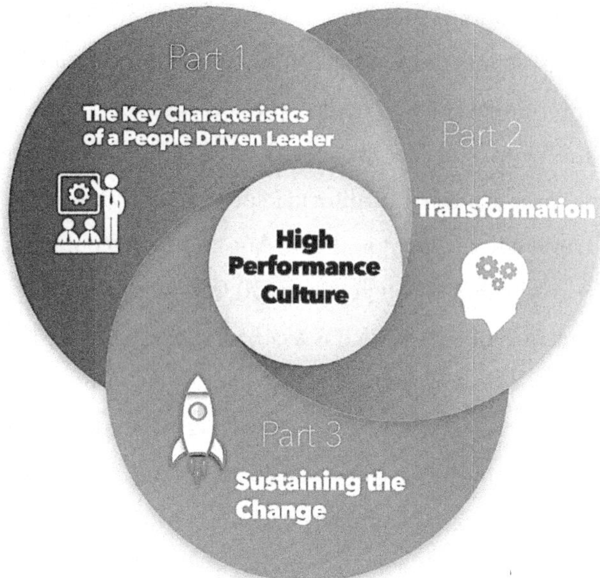

Questions for reflection and discussion appear throughout the book. Most appear at the end of chapters, and there are some mid-chapter questions as well. I encourage you to have a notebook close by while you read, and write down your answers to the questions. After you've considered what these questions might mean for you, share your answers with your team and discuss. Use these discussions as a launching point for a new conversation. The more you talk about what's possible, the more it becomes a possibility.

THE COST-BENEFIT TRADEOFF

Many of the decisions we make in 9-1-1 are motivated by keeping costs low. We'd hire more people, but we don't have the money. We'd send employees to training, but we can't afford it. We'd upgrade the equipment, but...

In essence we're saying, as the ship sinks, "We'd fix the hole, but we can't. There's no money."

Money is being spent, however, but not proactively. What we're really saying when we say we don't have the money to spend on prioritizing people is, "I don't see the value in spending money on this." We're too busy putting out fires (which costs lots of money). Where's the money going, and are there better, more intentional ways to deploy these resources?

One of the primary costs associated with the problems at the PSAP is overtime. One large center in California spent $3.51 million on overtime in 2016, nearly triple what it spent in 2011. Another large center, grappling with low morale, was burning through nearly 30,000 sick hours each year. At an average per hour rate of $30 (which is a conservative estimate for this center), this is $900,000 in lost work annually.

Then there's the cost of turnover. Some recruitment experts estimate the cost of replacing an employee to be 2 to 3 times the amount of their annual wage. At a 9-1-1 center, if a training program is 6 to 9 months long, and the trainee quits after they get through training, the cost is their salary, plus the salary of the instructor, plus the expense of finding a new candidate, PLUS the cost of the drag on morale when another trainee doesn't make it through.

And finally, there's the cost of civil litigation. When a center can't staff positions without overtime, things fall through the cracks. A burned-out operator may continually hang up on callers because he doesn't want to talk with them anymore. A stressed and fatigued dispatcher may miss a radio transmission and put officer safety at risk. Long hold times may lead to loss of life. A calltaker may misinterpret something while hastily trying to disposition a call and get onto the next.

In this highly litigious society, where millions are already spent by cities to settle lawsuits, 9-1-1 is likewise susceptible. In 2013, a county in Washington state paid a $2.3 million settlement after a citizen death. The 9-1-1 operator didn't properly upgrade the response priority on a call related to a shooting suspect. In a 2006 case out of Detroit, Michigan, two 9-1-1 call-takers were found personally liable for their actions on a call, after a large settlement was levied against the city. Just in the past 10 years, several other highly visible incidents have resulted in serious injury or death, in addition to costing the municipality involved millions of dollars.

The People Driven Leader takes ownership of these issues and works to correct them. As one director I interviewed said, "When things go wrong around here, it's my fault. If things go well, I congratulate my team for their hard work."

I first became interested in the power of this type of leadership while working as a 9-1-1 dispatcher for Los Angeles Police Department. One of the largest in the country, LAPD Communications Division employed over 600 employees at the time, with a cadre of 60 supervisors, and a management team of sworn sergeants and lieutenants overseen by a captain. During my 10-year career there, I was exposed to many different leadership styles. I noticed that, from the informal leaders to the supervisors all the way up to the captain, those who embodied a people driven approach were universally more successful than the others.

The People Driven Leaders, while in the minority, impacted the organization in positive and profound ways. It was under the leadership of one of these leaders that our entire division changed. Captain Joel Justice (his real name), upon assuming his 2-year post as Captain assigned Communications Division, began working to understand the challenges of the Division and targeting an area that might allow him to make the biggest positive impact. Using a people driven approach, at the end of his 24-month tenure, sick time usage had dropped by 45%.

One of the programs offered to employees during Capt. Justice's tenure was a weekly stress reduction session I designed and offered to my fellow coworkers. For 15 minutes once a week, my peers joined me to learn tools to de-stress. The same tools that had changed my life. This program ran for 18 months, and over 100 coworkers came through the sessions.

When I initially proposed the stress reduction sessions, Captain Justice simply said, "I'm all for it. Anything that can make life easier around here, I'll support."

This is an often-repeated theme emerging from People Driven Leaders. They are continually looking for ways to care for their people, and they aren't afraid to make changes in line with this personal mission. Captain Justice, by the virtue of putting his people first, made a positive impact in each of their lives.

From my own experience, and the experience of the People Driven Leaders I've worked with, transforming a 9-1-1 communications center isn't easy or quick. But it is possible, and now we understand how.

PART ONE

BEING THE TYPE OF LEADER THE CENTER NEEDS

CHAPTER 1
WHERE ARE ALL THE PEOPLE DRIVEN LEADERS?

Chris Conger, former Deputy Chief of Tucson Public Safety Communications Department in Tucson, Arizona, is a different kind of leader. I met Chief Conger at an APCO/NENA Conference and was impressed by what I learned. He genuinely cares about his people, and not in cursory way. He has made it a hallmark of his leadership style to show his staff that their welfare is important. He is present and available. He encourages his team and cheers them on. He openly communicates with all team members about the center's challenges and wins, mission and vision. He walks the floor, greets his team members when he arrives at the center, and invites them to share what's going on. He hears them out and uses these regular touchpoints as an opportunity to start conversations. Everyone feels involved in building a better organization. Things weren't always this rosy at Tucson Public Safety Communications.

In 2011, following a difficult transition to a new system, coupled with the tragic death of a 10-year-old girl, the mayor of Tucson moved responsibility of 9-1-1 communications from the General Services Department to the Fire Department. The after-action review identified several issues that led to the delay of service and resulting death. Training failures, an aging CAD, and a lack of leadership were top among these. The center was plagued by high turnover, low morale, and a feeling of anxiety about the schedule. A core issue was the lack of communication flow between management and line staff. The center's call processing times were twice the national standard on medical calls, and there was no unified sense of mission and goals.

Work schedules were the biggest hot button screaming for attention. After Communications was initially handed to Fire, a schedule change had been implemented. With the schedule change came anxiety over the 12-hour shift length, leading several employees to make complaints to councilmembers over their concerns. When Chief Conger came in, he put together a working group and tried to understand the schedule from a performance, call answering, and dispatch time perspective. They used the Erlang C formula and APCO Project RETAINS guidance and realized they couldn't switch to 8-hour or 10-hour shifts with their authorized staffing levels. A request for more positions was denied, so they designed a hybrid model, where sixteen people volunteered to work what they called "powershifts" of 12 hours, with other team members working shorter shifts.

Within a year of the handoff, things were looking better, but there were still opportunities for growth, including improvements in morale and culture. Appointed to the position in 2015, Chief Conger dove in quickly, immersing himself in the day-to-day at the center. After several months on the floor talking to people and trying to clearly understand the true problems and why people were anxious, a picture emerged. Speaking regularly with the center's informal leaders helped Conger further appreciate the center's culture situation. Chief Conger scheduled weekly meetings and established a trustworthy relationship with these informal leaders. "They would bring the rumors to the meetings, and we worked together to dispel the rumors," Chief Conger told me.

Conger's focus on improving communication really drove the change initiative. "Mission and vision matter," Conger says, "but it's the daily communication about why we do what we do that makes the biggest difference. How do we get better, provide better service, and get better each day?" Only by engaging people and asking powerful questions could solutions arise. To further encourage front line employees, Chief Conger empowered his supervisors to take an active role.

Prior to his arrival, supervisors weren't being used to their fullest potential. "In our monthly supervisor's meetings, I shared my expectations of them and my requirement that they delegate, empower and get to know their direct reports. I need to know about my people. If the supervisors aren't having these conversations, we don't know. Ultimately," Chief Conger told me, "we are a service industry, and the people who work for us need our support. They are taking care of the community, and we [the leadership team] need to be taking care of them."

Some supervisors ran with the opportunity to take additional initiative and loved the newly empowered approach. Other supervisors didn't. "Some folks are rule followers and can't see past the letter of the policy. We had to coach and mentor people to think outside the box and experiment," Chief Conger said. "One way we set this new standard for what was expected of supervisors was to create the Supervisor Certification class. Promotion-minded candidates would have to attend on their off-days, and they would learn about collective bargaining, legal issues, technology, and workforce management. After successful completion of the program, they would be certified to apply for supervisor. Some were still surprised by the amount of work when they got into the role, despite the certification. Some probationary appointees would wash out. The floor personnel would see this and knew the standard we were setting."

Chief Conger was well-suited for this assignment. Previously a union rep at the Fire Department, he had already developed a skill for working on employee concerns. His high level of emotional intelligence allowed him to deftly navigate the challenges posed by charged topics and tense exchanges. He found in many of his conversations with the staff that communication between management and line staff needed to improve. For being a team called "Communications," there wasn't much communicating taking place. Conger opened a dialogue about the schedule. He showed his front line supervisors the power of encouraging employees to bring forward new concepts and solutions to issues.

One of the biggest contributions Chief Conger made during his tenure was his focus on family. What do healthy functioning families do? The talk to each other, respect each other, and care about one another. This care flows through their exchanges and shows up as kindness in daily life. As Conger puts it, "We spend 52 hours a week with this family. We have ups and downs, high times and low times, but together, we save lives." With constructive communication as the rule, this "work family" was able to have disagreements and work through them together.

During his tenure, team members embraced Conger's actions—and began taking pride in the work again. "We went from 'We serve the Fire Department' to 'We're dispatchers and we own this,'" said Conger. The decrease in turnover and improvements in morale weren't the only metrics positively impacted. Call processing times dropped, and CPR outcomes improved. Through Conger's leadership, lives were literally saved, on both ends of the phone line. When a dispatcher feels good about their job and where they work, this is going to impact their home and family life as well.

People noticed his leadership efforts. In 2017, Deputy Chief Conger was named the Arizona NENA/APCO Director of the Year for his exemplary leadership.

CHAPTER 2
NOT A TECHNICAL "STAFFING" ISSUE BUT AN ADAPTIVE "PEOPLE" ISSUE

Unfortunately, the type of People Driven Leadership practiced by Deputy Chief Conger seems rare in our field. I found through my research that this was not only because of a scarcity in those possessing the necessary personal characteristics, but more notably because of deeper systemic issues within the 9-1-1 industry.

As I'll discuss in this section, we've been incorrectly diagnosing the causes of high turnover.

It's common in the 9-1-1 world to attribute high-turnover rates to low pay, the stress of the job, shift work, generational differences, and other external components. But this leads to incomplete solutions, and in fact, it exacerbates the problems because we do more of the same, hoping for a different result. "If the job is just the job," we think, "then there's nothing more I can do except keep hiring."

In other words, we think of these problems as technical issues that we can solve with better solutions. This leads us to look for leaders who have "technical" characteristics and skills. These qualities focus on the nuts and bolts of a job: a good technician is someone who can dispatch well, who is great at following policy and procedures, and who excels at dealing with the day-to-day processes of comm center life (like call-taking, dispatching, making sure equipment is upgraded and up-to-date) quickly and efficiently. Surely, these are important skills. They are also easy to measure and test for, which is why hiring processes tend to prioritize them.

Yet these are not the leadership qualities that create People Driven Centers, because employees with these characteristics are often ill-suited to address the issues at the *root* of high turnover.

In my 15+ years in the 9-1-1 industry, and as I specifically studied these high-performing centers, I realized that the problems facing our centers are not *staffing* issues; they are adaptive issues. To solve an adaptive issue, you need the right type of leader: a People Driven Leader.

The problem in the 9-1-1 industry is not just that we are not hiring and elevating People Driven Leaders like Deputy Chief Conger. It's also that we miss opportunities to bring such leaders into failing centers, because we often hire for the wrong attributes.

WHICH PRACTICES ARE MOST EFFECTIVE?

APCO's 2005 Project RETAINS (Responsive Efforts to Assure Integral Needs in Staffing) Effective Practices Guide provides a wealth of information on staffing and retention in public safety communications centers. Compiled after years of research with hundreds of participants from centers across the country, it offered the clearest understanding yet of the staffing challenges the 9-1-1 industry faced. The second Project RETAINS study, released in 2009, along with the supplemental 2018 study, "Staffing and Retention in Public Safety Answering Points," confirmed the challenges persist, and are worsening.

The Effective Practices Guide outlined the five most important factors when predicting center retention rates:

1. Staffing situation (whether the center is fully staffed)
2. Average overtime hours per month
3. Job complexity
4. Hourly base pay rate
5. Employee satisfaction with working conditions

Of these five factors, only two—job complexity and hourly base pay rate—are technical problems that require a relatively straightforward approach.

Technical problems are easy to identify. They often lend themselves to quick and easy solutions that an authority or expert can administer. Their solutions generally require change in just one or a few places, and the changes are often contained within organizational boundaries. People are generally receptive to technical solutions, and, as a result, they can often be implemented quickly. Technical leaders are often proficient at solving these technical problems.

If I, as a leader who takes pride in my technical proficiency, believe the hourly base pay at my center is too low, I can conduct a pay analysis, and then, based on the analysis, raise the pay. If we determine that overall job complexity is driving people to quit, we can redesign the job, rewrite the description, and reduce the complexity relatively easily.

Yet, focusing on the technical leaves the other three challenges on the table: staffing situation, average overtime and employee satisfaction. These are what I call *adaptive challenges.*

Adaptive challenges are different. They require different solutions and sometimes a completely different mindset than technical problems. First, they are difficult to identify and easy to deny. They require changes in values, beliefs, roles, relationships and approaches to work. People immersed in the problem have to do the work to solve it. They require change in numerous places, and usually across organizational boundaries. People resist acknowledging adaptive challenges; the solutions require experimentation and discovery; and they can take a long time to implement. Finally, you cannot force the solutions upon the members of the organization. Their implementation requires a specific leadership approach.

My grandfather was 36 years old when he experienced a heart attack. Quadruple bypass surgery and medication helped save him in the short-term, but no technical fix could release Grandpa from his own responsibility for changing the habits of a lifetime. He had to *adapt*. Grandpa had to stop smoking, improve his diet, get some exercise, and take time to relax, remembering to breathe deeply each day. Grandpa's doctor could provide sustaining *technical expertise* and take supportive action, but only Grandpa could *adapt* his ingrained habits to improve his long-term health.

The doctor faced the leadership task of mobilizing the patient to make critical behavioral changes; Grandpa faced the adaptive work of figuring out which specific changes to make and how to incorporate them into his daily life.

Three of the biggest issues facing every comm center, as identified in the Effective Practices Guide, are adaptive challenges: they point back to each other in a circular fashion (the staffing situation leads to more OT hours, which leads to dissatisfaction with working conditions, which leads back to staffing challenges).

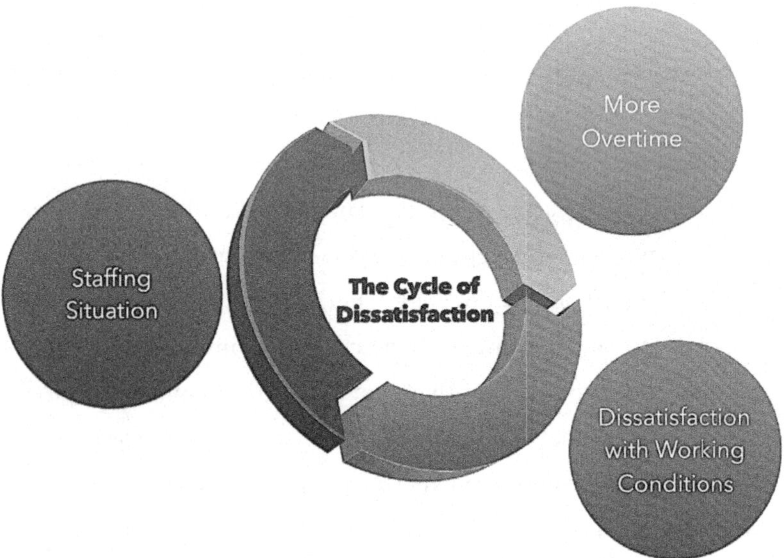

Going from your center's status quo to high performance culture is an adaptive challenge. No amount of technical quick-fix can solve deep-seated issues around communication, accountability, and relationships. This requires strong leadership.

People Driven Leaders are well-suited to address adaptive challenges because they are more attuned to the emotional dimension of organizational life. A People Driven Leader is constantly tending to the people side of work life, asking questions, soliciting solutions, and generally staying in conversation with team members. As a result of this genuine care for what their people are thinking and feeling, this type of leader has much more power to influence and empower their people.

Unfortunately, our industry tends to prioritize technical experience over people skills. So often a supervisory promotion is granted to the most tenured dispatcher—someone great at the job but not necessarily imbued with leadership ability. Unfortunately for the centers who make this mistake, many skilled technicians are this way at the expense of their people skills. They've kept their heads down and practiced what they know best: working the console. Without people skills, one is much less equipped to lead. People skills only come by working with people, something many 9-1-1 professionals cringe at (including many in supervisory roles!).

In contrast, my research demonstrates that technical experience matters only to a certain degree. Yes, a working knowledge of the center's functions can aid in a leader's effectiveness, but what's lacking in technical knowledge can be sourced from existing staff by the leader. A technician is afraid to admit when they don't know something; they worry what this says about them. An adaptive leader, however, uses opportunities like this to bring the team together.

I spoke with a center in Texas confronted with a staffing crisis, who had gone searching for new leadership. They hired an amazing candidate, who had worked in several communications centers previously, along with working leadership roles in private industry. Because of her experience *outside* the 9-1-1 industry, she knew what was possible when it came to employee engagement and satisfaction. Her organizational experience in 9-1-1 meant that she had a vision of how to bring this expertise to her new comm center.

Conversely, a comm center manager or director with technical expertise may be overly identified with this expertise. It is all they know, and this knowledge has served them well in the past. When assigned to a new center, this manager uses their one-size-fits-all approach to make swift changes at the new center. They make these changes without consulting the staff because it's worked in the past, and they are the "expert." When this happens, frustration abounds. The manager gets frustrated because there's no easy solution, and the employees get frustrated because the attempted solution didn't work AND they still have problems (plus, they were never consulted).

As Ronald Heifetz says in his book *The Practice of Adaptive Leadership: Tools and Tactics for Changing Your Organization and the World*, "The most common leadership failure stems from trying to apply technical solutions to adaptive challenges."

If three of the five ***most important factors*** affecting your center's retention are adaptive challenges that don't have easy solutions, what do we do? We must begin the difficult task of understanding these adaptive challenges and then implementing solutions. Remember, these three factors are related:

1. Staffing situation (whether the center is fully staffed)
2. Average overtime hours per month
3. Employee satisfaction with working conditions

As we improve one, the others follow.

Going deeper into the Effective Practices Guide (EPG), we see that the authors explored the factor "employee satisfaction" more deeply. Their findings, cited below, highlight the complexity of adaptive challenges.

From the EPG:

> Our definition of employee satisfaction in public safety communications centers is the degree to which employees feel content about a constellation of issues: the **recognition** they receive for their work, the **quality** of their interactions with management and co-workers, the **physical**

environment where they work, their **schedule** and the scheduling process, the **salary** and **benefits**, and the adequacy of the initial and ongoing **training** that is provided.

When we fail to take these elements into consideration, we see the organizational challenges that are considered the norm in 9-1-1. Staffing issues, low morale, negativity, mandatory OT, sick time abuse, trainee washout, inability to recruit excellent candidates, worker's compensation claims, poor call service levels, citizen complaints, slow response times, and more are what we come to expect.

Employee satisfaction matters a lot and affects all the others, and unfortunately for those in a leadership role, it is the most nebulous. It's all about the "soft" side of work life: the human element. In an attempt to quantify this, the Effective Practices Guide went so far as to outline eight factors that predicted employee satisfaction:

1. Center performance (a composite score made up of multiple items)
2. Preparation and ongoing training (also a composite score)
3. Feeling appreciated by management
4. Employee satisfaction with the shift selection process
5. Effective mentoring of new trainees
6. Feeling appreciated by their immediate supervisor
7. A thorough and extensive application and screening process
8. Feeling appreciated by the media

If you look carefully, you'll see a theme emerge, with both the definition of employee satisfaction and the factors above: it's all about how your center's staff *feels*.

Do they feel prepared for the job (training)? Do they feel appreciated? Do they feel satisfied with the shifts? Do the trainees feel cared for (mentoring)? Do they feel confident in being a right fit (application and screening)? Project

RETAINS, while offering great information and tools to use when it comes to calculating your staffing needs, turnover rate, employee availability and other technical metrics, doesn't offer any concrete advice or steps on how to make your employees feel like coming into work tomorrow.

The most important factors determining your center's retention depend on how satisfied your employees *feel*. This satisfaction is tempered by a confluence of a variety of elements, which also hinge on a feeling. Center performance—the number one factor predicting employee satisfaction—largely deals with how employees feel about supervision and management.

If it all hinges on how our organizations make the people who work in them *feel,* there's a disconnect in the fact that 9-1-1 is an industry whose tenured employees live by the mantra "Suck it up, buttercup" when it comes to discussing feelings. This is very likely part of the problem.

Another part of the problem is that it's much easier to be a technician than it is to be a People Driven Leader. To the technician, the "softer" side of work life is infuriating. A technician wants to make an organizational change and have everything snap into place with no further fuss. The technician sees a simple problem, like sick time abuse, and suggests a simple solution: require employees to bring a doctor's note in every time they use a sick day. But for employees so dissatisfied with the way things are, requiring a sick note won't prevent them from using sick time. They'll just go to the doctor anyway or find another workaround.

"Write them up, discipline and then fire them," the technician says—a simple solution to the disengaged worker, except when you can't quickly fire them or even afford to lose the body. Aside from the obvious downsides to firing people except as a very last resort, when has the "whack-a-mole" approach ever worked as an approach to engaging disgruntled employees?

Simple fixes do not work in today's 9-1-1 communications centers. We can't discipline our way to improved employee satisfaction. We need to establish people driven initiatives and devotion to making positive changes. It's ok to be focused on metrics, but we have to measure the right things while looking at the total picture. Creating high performance culture requires careful attention to the soft stuff. However, just because it's soft doesn't mean it can't be quantified.

AN ADAPTIVE FIX TO A TECHNICAL CHALLENGE

From the outset, it seems like Chief Conger and Tucson Fire Communications faced a technical challenge. CPR call processing times were high, affecting CPR saves. To address this technical issue, we might do a few things:

1. Write a new policy outlining the punishment for processing calls too slowly
2. Circulate a department-wide order reminding staff of current policy and have every employee sign for the order, indicating they've been notified
3. Publicly post call processing times for all to see
4. Hire more people
5. Reprimand low performers and begin progressive discipline

Each of these potential solutions fails to address a deeper issue that formal discipline, additional notifications, and hiring more people can't. Chief Conger understood the deeper issue and provided an adaptive solution. He offered training classes that taught the "why" behind quick and efficient handling of CPR calls. The team learned about anatomy and what happens to the body in a short amount of time (heart tissue begins to die within four minutes). Based on this "why," the training classes encouraged more assertiveness and quickness. Once they had this foundational knowledge in place, the center began measuring call processing times by person, shift and team. This increased ownership of the process, as every team member appreciated the role they played in the life-saving family. Call processing times fell by 50%, and CPR outcomes improved.

A People Driven Leader understands employee motivation in a way other managers do not. He or she knows employees don't respond well to carrots and sticks. They are generally intelligent and want to do well in the job they've chosen. A People Driven Leader knows they can believe one of two things about their employees:

1. They want to come to work and can thrive if given the tools to do so; or,
2. They need to be coerced with force or fear.

This kind of leader chooses to believe the first. They also know that what they choose to believe will show up in every one of their actions, words and reactions. It will condition whether you go to bat for your employees or keep things the way they are. Your belief on this point will determine whether you are a leader or a manager.

CHAPTER 3
PEOPLE DRIVEN LEADERSHIP IS THE KEY TO AN ADAPTIVE APPROACH

In my research, I noticed some key characteristics all People Driven Leaders share that make them uniquely qualified to tackle the adaptive challenges facing our centers. I call them **The Five Key Characteristics**, and they are:

1. Exhibiting emotional intelligence
2. Inspiring values, or knowing what you stand for
3. An ability to set the bar and articulate clear expectations
4. A commitment to excellence, or continual improvement
5. The ability to inspire trust

The 5 Key Characteristics

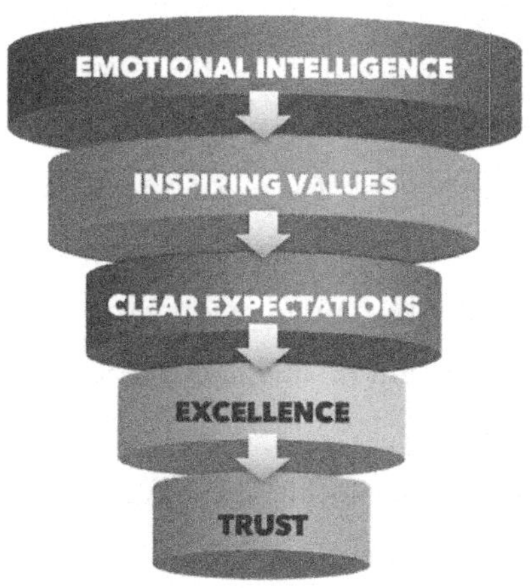

Through the application of these five characteristics, People Driven Leaders show up in service of the front line, driving results that are far better than the industry average.

I'll walk through each of these qualities in the sections that follow. If you're reading this book, you've likely been tasked with the difficult goal of helping turn around a struggling comm center or to "level-up" an already strong operation.

My goal is to help you understand how to identify each of these qualities in others, whether they be potential or current co-workers, so you can build a strong team to advance your important mission. I also hope that you will be able to use this book as a guide to develop these characteristics in yourself, so you can best contribute to your key role in your team.

KNOW THYSELF AND OTHERS: THE POWER OF EMOTIONAL INTELLIGENCE

People Driven Leaders are perfectly suited to address adaptive challenges because of how attuned they are to the emotional dimension of work life. This intelligence prompts them to ask the question, "How do I want to feel coming into work?" They then seek to create that feeling for themselves, and for the people under their charge.

Coined "emotional intelligence" in the mid-90s, those possessing this quality are able to make work life more livable for everyone around them. As Daniel Goleman said in his book *Emotional Intelligence*, "Some of the reasons [why emotional intelligence is important] are patently obvious—imagine the consequences for a team [in the comm center, for example] when someone is unable to keep from exploding in anger or has no sensitivity about what the people around him are feeling." When we're upset, we make bad decisions and say things we later regret (and in this industry, it's sometimes on a recorded line). Said in another way: stress makes us dumb, and without understanding the impact on our emotional makeup, life for ourselves and our coworkers can be even more challenging.

In their book *Emotional Intelligence 2.0*, Drs. Travis Bradberry and Jean Greaves define emotional intelligence as one's ability to recognize and understand your emotions in yourself and others, and your ability to use this awareness to manage your behavior and relationships. Emotional intelligence is a rather intangible "something" in each of us. It affects how we manage behavior, navigate social complexities, and make personal decisions that achieve positive results.

Through the administration of over 500,000 emotional intelligence assessments, Drs. Bradberry and Greaves have found that your emotional intelligence quotient (or EQ, for short) is so critical to personal success that it accounts for 58% of performance in all types of jobs. A closer look at the four skills demonstrated by those with high EQ highlights why it's so important for life in a comm center.

The first skill associated with EQ is **self-awareness**, which is the ability to recognize and understand your moods, emotions and drives, as well as their effect on others. Self-awareness comes from knowing your strengths and weaknesses and understanding their impact on your daily life. While it's easiest to spot low self-awareness in others (they frequently blame others for their shortcomings), noticing where *you're* at offers the most gains, in both your personal and professional life.

The second skill is **self-management**, which is what you do with your awareness. It's the ability to control or redirect disruptive impulses and moods, the propensity to suspend judgement—in short, to think before acting. Vitally important in the comm center, self-management allows us to think before we speak, pause before responding, and create space around our habitual reflexive patterns. Many comm centers are reduced to living with perpetually low morale because of the lack of self-management. The tenured employees tend to set this standard, frequently offering as an excuse for their rough demeanor,

"I don't sugarcoat, I just tell it like it is—suck it up, if you don't like it." While some may appreciate this "direct" approach, most do not. Without the third skill—social awareness—it's nearly impossible to know who you're dealing with and modulate your communication approach accordingly.

Social awareness is the ability to understand other people's emotional makeup and the skill of knowing how to treat people according to their emotional reactions (empathy). With empathy we can walk in another's shoes. The best leaders in this profession use social awareness to take the whole person into account when navigating discipline conversations, making everyday contact and reading the room. If you've ever walked into the comm center and noticed that something was up (two people were at war, something difficult was being discussed, or some other vibe was creating a funk in the room—even though no one said anything about it), you've tapped your social awareness. The antidote to the one-size-fits-all communication approach, social awareness builds bonds of emotional connection throughout the team.

The fourth skill is **relationship management**, or social skills. This is proficiency in managing relationships and building networks, along with an ability to find common ground and build rapport. Social skills arise out of what you do with your self- and social awareness.

Each skill builds on and informs the last. When you're able to prioritize and grow these skills, greater levels of team camaraderie and cohesion at the comm center result. It's interesting to note how the skills are arranged and how they work together. It all begins with you: self-awareness. Without knowing yourself—your strengths, weaknesses, triggers, and how others' emotions affect you—it's easy to get caught in the blame game. In fact, people with low self-awareness may feel powerless to change anything dissatisfying in their lives. They are a ship tossed about on turbulent seas, a victim of the weather and the waves.

Self-Assessment

Understanding how your mood affects the team is a key skill of emotional intelligence. Leaders who have a positive attitude are much better equipped to lead in the perpetually negative environment of a communications center.

1. How might your mood affect your role at work?
2. How does your mood affect your energy level at work?
3. Are you always aware of your mood and its impact on your work?
4. What can you do to improve your awareness or your impact on the people around you?

Becky Bacon, Director at Christian County Emergency Services in Missouri, is highly emotionally intelligent. Hired in 2016 as Deputy Director to handle day-to-day operations at her medium-sized comm center, she used her people driven approach to completely change her new center's culture. Though they had never been fully-staffed, they hoped it was possible. Past experience proved otherwise, but it didn't deter Becky from trying. She really cared about making a difference at her center; so, she took the time to look at the deeper issues creating the center's problems.

She began by talking to her people. She got to know them. She learned about their motivations, their strengths and weaknesses. She found that some didn't know what they were "meant to do." Young employees couldn't see where they needed to go because they'd never been shown before. Becky took it upon herself to show them, in terms they could understand and respect.

It took a year of sitting down with her people, asking questions, and insisting on consistency before she really started making changes. Prior to Becky's appointment, some supervisors did things their own way, creating confusion throughout the organization. They would share the information they wanted to share and in the way they wanted to share it, without regard for the receiver of the message, or acceptable procedure. This behavior persisted because it hadn't been addressed before.

The supervisors were trained on how to communicate effectively. Further, Becky demonstrated this aptitude for communicating with tact and sincerity so others could model it. Over time, the old habits changed, allowing the changes Becky was implementing to take root. And because her employees felt she had invested in them *before* attempting changes, she had built the foundational trust that enabled changes to take place.

As the changes unfolded, Becky maintained strong communication with her staff. Her goal was to be transparent at all times. Transparency through communication was just one aspect of Becky's overarching personal mission, which was going the extra mile for her people. This exemplary leader knows that you can have the best equipment, but if you don't have the people—and they aren't trained and happy—it doesn't matter at all. As she said in our conversation, "We all have 'too much' work to do. You must be willing to take the time to get the right person in the right place. We're all going to fail otherwise."

With this philosophy guiding her daily actions, Becky succeeded. Within 16 months of coming into the organization, the center was fully-staffed. The journey was not without its challenging conversations. At times, they found they had to cut their losses and let a new hire go.

In one situation, a conversation with a "problem child" who seemed to be on her way out offered an amazing turnaround. Prior to the conversation, the employee would frequently ruin the mood for everyone on the shift. She would throw her bag down at the console, breathe audible sighs during and after calls, slam the phone down, and demonstrate an attitude that clearly expressed, "I don't want to be here." During the conversation, Becky acknowledged the problem, and instead of telling the employee to "shape up or ship out," she couched it as follows: "We have a problem, and we need to do something about it." By using "we" instead of "you," Becky invited the employee into a mutually beneficial problem-solving conversation and gave her a forum to explain the challenges she faced on her own terms. This led them to agree on a course of action. The "problem child" made an amazing change and received the 2017 Director's Award for the center.

The transition Becky oversaw could not have been possible without her emotional intelligence. Adeptly navigating the difficult conversations that were the norm during her first year in the role required all four skills, firing on all cylinders. Her self-awareness allowed her to identify and refine her strengths as a leader and communicator. Her self-management helped her maintain her positive attitude amidst the challenges faced. As she said, "It's really about the attitude—a happy, healthy attitude creates the aptitude." With social awareness, she could empathize with her team members, allowing them to feel heard again. And by tapping into her social skills and focusing on relationship building, Becky was able to get to know her people, build rapport and find common ground. If she had lacked any of these skills, Becky's attempt at staffing her center would've likely failed—like so many before.

Our comm centers are changing more quickly than ever, and the technology is only one part of it. The most challenging aspect lies in the people side of the business. Only a certain type of person can navigate the generational differences, as well as the different educational and cultural backgrounds, while motivating and inspiring everyone.

FROM EMOTIONAL INTELLIGENCE FLOWS VALUES

As the first skill required to build emotional intelligence, self-awareness is also the core of leadership. Without being self-aware, it's impossible to be an effective leader in any comm center position (lead, instructor, supervisor—anything). How can one hope to lead others if they don't know how to lead themselves?

People Driven Leaders are self-aware and know where they are going and why. They have a vision and know what fuels it. The fuel for a leader's bold action is a deep knowledge of what they stand for, and they express this through the leadership values they hold most dear. Rooted in these values, this type of leader is guided to do the right thing, especially when it's difficult. In every interview for this book, I was struck by the leader's resolve. They were passionately driven to make a difference for those under their charge. Devoted to this personal mission, they each embraced a willingness to address issues previously left untouched.

Melissa Alterio, Director with Roswell Public Safety Dispatch in Roswell, Georgia, stepped into her role in 2015. She inherited a situation left by the previous director, who had vacated the position ten months earlier. Melissa immediately became present and involved. She noticed the team had lost hope. The center felt broken and defeated. One of the biggest challenges she faced was the conduct of the communications manager, who had been in the role for two years. Melissa began holding the manager accountable for the responsibilities of the role, as dictated by the job description.

Faced with this new level of scrutiny, the manager began taking more and more time off, and eventually left. Upon the manager's departure, Melissa's team expressed shock. They said, "You never let on that there were problems, or that you were doing anything about the problem." After addressing the deeper issues—including sick time abuse and other behaviors that had always been a part of life at this center—Melissa saw hope return to her team's eyes.

Melissa deliberately didn't complain to her staff about the host of issues she faced. In fact, she spent the first six months of her tenure listening and learning. She knew she couldn't bring about lasting change if she didn't understand things from her new team's perspective. This willingness to put her ego aside to understand what the center needed—instead of using her previous experience to *assume* what it needed—is a hallmark of a People Driven Leader. Many who are appointed an executive leadership role at a center are quick to make changes—to "make their mark." These rapid actions, often taken without consulting the team, fail to prevent people from leaving. On the contrary, they usually drive good people out of the organization.

A willingness to listen quietly to the real issues stems from humility. The paramilitary patrol-centric model rewards assertiveness and a willingness to "take control." But this approach doesn't work in the comm center. Dispatchers are family-oriented. Families work on behalf of the whole, often putting themselves aside for the good of the family. To do this, one must be humble.

Lisa Davet, another leader I spoke with, exemplifies this trait. This Assistant Director with Chagrin Valley Regional Dispatch in Ohio said, "I don't even see myself as a leader," despite the fact that Lisa was the driving force behind creating a culture that continually attracts and retains great people. One recent addition to the Chagrin Valley team said to me, "I love it here, and I haven't been able to say that before." Unfortunately, not many comm center employees *can* or *would* say this.

The values mentioned above—humility, accountability, and understanding—aren't the only leadership values that matter, obviously, and the values that truly matter are those that help the leader make life easier for the people they serve. The tough work of being this type of leader—one who loses sleep over whether they're making the right decisions for their people—begins with introspection. If you haven't considered what you stand for and the lengths you'll go to live by these personal standards, this is a great place to begin.

In the classic leadership book *The Leadership Challenge*, authors James Kouzes and Barry Posner outline the five qualities of exemplary leadership. After examining 70,000 responses to their 1987 study, Kouzes and Posner found that exemplary leaders across a wide swath of industries had certain distinct qualities in common. The first pertains to the actions the leader takes and from where these actions flow. According to the book, the first practice of exemplary leaders is *modeling the way*. Said another way, they walk their talk. So many in supervisory positions don't embody this first practice, and as a result, don't inspire followers. And as the popular saying goes, "A leader without followers is simply a person going for a walk."

We've all worked for a boss whose motto seems to be, "Do as I say, not as I do." One communications manager spent mornings eating his breakfast at his desk while reading the paper—for hours—in a windowed office visible by the team working the dispatch floor. His team members were working forced overtime every day, while this manager came in late, left early, and spent hours each day lazing about. What message does this send? What way is this manager modeling?

As mentioned above, the first practice isn't about the people under your charge. In order to effectively model the way, you must know yourself. The quickest pathway to this personal understanding is to examine your closely held values. What values do you stand for? What is your leadership philosophy?

Once you've determined your values as a leader, it's important to live by them and articulate them to your team. The leadership team at Chagrin Valley Regional Dispatch includes Director Nick DiCicco, Assistant Director Lisa Davet and a team of supervisors across two centers providing services for 32 municipalities. Lisa and Nick work every day to inspire and maintain a culture based on strong family values. They welcome their people into the group before they even start their job. They sit out on the floor regularly. They go out with the team after work. They work daily to show the respect and appreciation that any healthy family relationship requires.

Christine Mayzzeo recently joined the Chagrin Valley team as a front line telecommunicator. She had worked at four other centers before and was wary of joining another because of her previous experience. Her apprehension disappeared after meeting Lisa. "I felt welcomed by her, even before I started," Christine shared during our conversation. That feeling of inclusion grew when Christine started working the floor. "I didn't feel like an outsider," she continued. "I was immediately included in conversations—like I had been there all along. Almost right away, I was encouraged to join in a contest, so I participated. It's clear we're all part of the family, and we can talk about anything."

Leadership at Chagrin Valley has a habit of making deposits into the relationship bank account with each employee, every day. This is a leadership team who knows, a) without building relationships first, there won't be enough trust for changes to take root, and b) no one cares about what you know until they know how much you care – just like in a family. Yes, you can issue a "direct order" and force people to comply, or attempt to discipline them into compliance, but the results are usually better when you inspire people to get on board of their own volition.

Leadership is all about relationships. You can't get anything done without everyone else, especially in the comm center. When you take the time to build relationships with each person by sitting down with them and trying to understand things from their perspective, only then can you begin articulating your vision. By making it all about them first and the vision second, you're much more likely to succeed. Employees will invest at a much deeper level. They will work to change things for *themselves*. The first step can take several months. It takes a while to build the trusting relationships of a family. After the family comes together, it's time to set some goals for the future of the center, based on the shared values of center staff and the compelling future vision.

A leader with clear values is better able to find her voice. The leader's "why" flows from such values, and when the leader articulates them, it allows her team the choice to follow or not. Shared values are like the connective tissue of an organization.

Clarity around shared values ensures that everyone is on the same page, and we're all working for the same thing.

But it must always begin with the leader and what they stand for.

Self-Assessment

1. What values are most important to you in your leadership role?
2. How do these values animate your personal leadership behavior (i.e., what's a specific *action* you take that flows from one of your deepest values)?
3. What's something that ignites your passion? How can you bring more of this passion to your leadership role?

FROM VALUES FLOWS EXPECTATIONS

By clearly understanding their values and what these values mean to the organization, People Driven Leaders are able to form and articulate clear expectations for themselves and the team. Only by communicating what their values mean from an organizational perspective can a leader inspire a set of shared values that really carry weight.

In 2009, Grand Junction Regional Communications Center in Grand Junction, Colorado, found themselves in a tough place. Leadership had taken a sobering look at the conditions and realized the center had become unbearable. The statistics on trainee turnover reflected this feeling, with 50-75% of trainees leaving before completing the program. HR exit interviews told of horrible mistreatment, as tenured staff bullied and intimidated newer members of the team, and training instructors thumped trainees on the top of the head with a pen to get them to perform more quickly.

The assistant manager at the time, Monica Million, had previously worked in private industry and knew there was a possibility of creating an organization in which people enjoyed working. She knew how people wanted to be treated—how *she* would want to be treated. Her care and attention formed the foundation for what came next. During a series of team meetings, the entire 50-person team got together and answered the question, "How do we want to treat each other?" Respect, integrity and teamwork were the shared values that flowed from these conversations.

Discovering and then explicitly stating what your center stands for is a powerful exercise. Every word, action and behavior thereafter is either in alignment with the stated values or not. It's easy to set clear expectations when everyone has bought-in to such foundational purpose.

The expectation moving forward at Grand Junction was that every employee—manager, supervisor, admin, line-level, alike—would treat each other with respect, act with integrity, and embrace teamwork, every single day. Supervisors were held accountable for ensuring employees acted in accordance with these values. The staff was likewise empowered to hold supervisors and peers accountable. Everyone agreed, from the outset, to have one-on-one conversations with each other to foster this accountability. Collectively, the members of the team had drawn a line in the sand: "This is what we require," everyone agreed, "or you'll be held to account."

The clear expectations set the bar, and with everyone's help—flowing from the top-down, from the button-up and across—things started to shift. Several team members decided to leave during this transition, deciding the job was no longer for them. Others had to be disciplined out of the organization. Clearly stated values that team members speak about frequently, along with the expectations that follow them, have a polarizing effect. People are either on board, or they aren't. No hard feelings.

What might've happened if the old behavior continued after defining these shared values? Things might've stayed the same, or more likely, gotten worse. Nothing erodes trust more than a manager saying they're going to do something (like espouse the value of integrity) and not follow through. The implicit message is that it's ok for everyone else to do the same.

People Driven Leaders set clear expectations based on the organization's shared values because they know who they are and why they do what they do.

Self-Assessment

1. How do your leadership values flow into the expectations you communicate to your team? For example, if integrity and accountability are among your top values, how often are you communicating expectations with these values in mind?
2. Where could you be clearer about your expectations, from this values-driven standpoint?

COMMITMENT TO FINDING THE BEST WAY: EXCELLENCE

When a leader has a clear understanding of who they are (EQ) and what they stand for (values), their consistency around values-oriented expectations leads to organizational excellence. Also known as quality through continuous improvement, excellence is the ongoing pursuit of the **best way to do the work**. A People Driven Leader knows the work is never done. The antidote to the "same old way," this commitment is essential during difficult transitions, when getting everyone on the same page is a key precursor to producing industry-best results.

Lynn Bowler, a 38-year veteran of 9-1-1 based in Elk Grove, California, has seen the industry change a lot during her career. In fact, when she started in 1980, 9-1-1 wasn't even in effect in California yet! During her tenure as Support Services Manager for Elk Grove PD, Lynn oversaw the transition from Elk Grove being a contract city with the local sheriff's office to becoming its own PD. Her responsibility was to bring dispatch, records and evidence together under one roof.

From the outset, Lynn told the Chief that it was going to be more difficult to hire 18 dispatchers than it would be to hire 100 cops. "We had no real identity and different cultural expectations," Lynn said. "Bringing sheriff's deputies, Elk Grove Police and contract employees all to the same table was going to be challenging, from every perspective." To navigate this challenge, Lynn asked for help.

They developed a hiring process with a consultant's assistance, and together defined questions and had conversations. They talked about culture, shift rotation, and seniority. A transition team of 5 or 6 helped develop policy around the conversations, establishing a foundation. Lynn's role throughout the process was to insure development of leadership, and lead from behind.

Quality through continuous improvement was always Lynn's approach, long after the initial stages of the transition were complete. "There's always more we can do," Lynn said in our conversation. "We've tweaked shift rotation and assignments many times, because that's how the team wants it. You really have to stop and listen to your people."

When change is the norm and the pace of change is quickening, it's better to embrace it, drive it and use it to improve the organization. "Be creative with problem-solving," Lynn explains, "and don't be afraid to make changes. Look for ways to develop processes that are fairer, and never say, 'This is just how we do it.'"

When I asked Lynn about how she combatted the biggest challenges faced by her comm center (attrition, low morale, staffing, etc.), her response was interesting and truly spoke to her commitment to finding the best way: "We've never had to quantify the cost of these things. We always knew that making changes would have an effect on them, so that's what we've done," she said. "Our willingness to deviate from a patrol-centric model has been important."

The People Driven Leader is committed to finding the best way. She is always experimenting and taking risks. She makes the time to ask her people what they think and seeks input on how to make things better.

Monica Million exemplified this commitment while at Grand Junction Regional Communications Center. The change initiative began in 2009 and gained traction quickly. By 2011, the center achieved a goal they had set as a target from the outset: they were named Best Communications Center by APCO/NENA Colorado 2011. But even though they had come a long way, Monica soon found the transformation wasn't complete.

The center's morale started slipping again in 2012. As Operations Manager by this time, Monica took action. "We had to sit and write down our expectations of each team and workgroup," Monica explained. "Telecommunicators, supervisors and managers each shared their expectations up, down and across the organization. Then we posted these expectations on the wall, further clarifying what our values meant to us and how we expected these shared values to show up in daily work life."

This kept people who completed the training program in the job, but there were still problems. The final turn was to address hiring and recruitment. Despite all the work they'd done up until this point—four years since the 2009 beginning—Grand Junction still had 30-50% turnover in trainees. Committed to finding a better way, management revamped the hiring process and changed the training approach. Monica shared the #1 thing that worked: "turning the CTOs into teachers, getting them training on how to effectively reach adult learners, and empowering them with the responsibility of their trainee's success." Creating ownership of the training process and equipping CTOs with the tools to succeed caused them to engage the process at a deep and personal level.

After 5 years of trying different things, peeling back each subsequent layer of the onion, Grand Junction Regional Communications Center had just 6% annual turnover, and only through promotion and transfer. During the same time period, they achieved 100% retention in trainees.

People Driven Leaders understand that the road to excellence may be a long and difficult one. But with clearly-articulated expectations holding the team together, they are willing to make the journey.

Shannon Price, Director at Sugar Land Public Safety Dispatch in the Houston, TX area, worked to improve retention at her center for years before her efforts were rewarded. When she stepped into the Director role, the turnover rate hovered near 20%. The year after that, it jumped to 37%. The next year, 32%. During these three years, Shannon was hard at work, searching for the right leadership team, implementing a mentoring program, and holding people accountable for their actions. Two negative supervisors resigned or were terminated during this time. In the fourth year, things shifted. The center posted a retention rate of 100%. They had become a People Driven Center.

Similar to the situation in Grand Junction, Shannon didn't stop at zero turnover. She turned her attention to the center's trainee success rate, knowing that it wasn't where it needed to be. The center hired an ops manager in charge of recruitment, hiring and the training program. Having one person dedicated to these functions prompted the trainee success rate to improve. Within 2 years, it hit 90%, up from just 50%. Shannon still works daily to inspire a culture of innovation, where her team attempts solutions, refines them and tries again.

A People Driven Leader's commitment to finding the best way is rooted in her "why." As Monica Million put it, "We have invested a great deal of money in people who truly believe their job is a higher purpose. We need to give them tools to succeed."

Giving your employees the tools to succeed seems like a no-brainer. Of course, you're going to give them what they need, right!? But not all centers do, and further, some may not know what the right tools even are. Faulty or failing equipment, no breaks, untrained supervisors, and managers or directors who are absent all constitute a lack of the tools required for a successful center.

Without giving personnel the tools, training and support they need to succeed, it's hard for a leader to embody the fourth quality.

Self-Assessment

1. What area of your comm center is in need of a new way of doing things? Where has "this is the way we've always done it" prevented positive change from happening?
2. What is a commitment you can make today to find the better way?

Bringing together your leadership team and discussing the questions throughout this chapter is a great way to begin charting the way forward. In the leadership training classes and team building sessions my company offers, getting clear on these important questions is a huge part of the work.

CREATING OWNERSHIP AND BUY-IN: INSPIRING TRUST

The fifth quality flows from all the rest. An emotionally intelligent leader is attuned to their people's emotional and fundamental needs, and intuitively builds relationships that lift people up. These connections make it much easier for the leader to communicate the values for which they stand and foster buy-in. People Driven Leaders inspire trust by setting expectations, holding people to those expectations and then meeting expectations (excellence). When expectations are communicated and then met in an ongoing, consistent and visible way, it creates a culture of trust.

In 2010, Polk County Communications faced a massive undertaking. Consolidation with Polk County Sheriff's Office would bring their current staffing from 64 positions to 145. Morale issues, turnover and sick time abuse were already a concern at both centers, so making a smooth transition to one center seemed nearly impossible. A new computer-aided dispatch (CAD) system and operational protocols further complicated matters, and the short timeline for completion meant the pressure was on.

Ivan Whitaker, the dispatch manager who oversaw the consolidation, knew he couldn't do it alone, or force compliance. He was going to need everyone on board with the mission. "If I was going to be successful," Ivan said, "it had to go through the employees. If I couldn't foster ownership and buy-in, I couldn't meet objectives."

For the first two months of the consolidation effort, Ivan met with each employee individually (yes, every single one.) He asked them what they thought about the current state of affairs. He inquired into the issues and wrote them down. Ivan and his team ranked the issues based on these initial meetings, and from the ranking system, he understood what to tackle first. Once they'd conducted the interviews and collected the information, then what?

"Most [managers] don't take it further," Ivan notes. "Many at the center had grown disillusioned with management and didn't believe I'd do anything more. Employees generally thought, 'Nothing I say will [make a difference], so what's the point?' I had to assure them it would make a difference, and then I had to follow through."

Communication turned out to be the biggest issue at Polk County. There had been a dictatorship, with management and supervision preventing the flow of information to all in the organization. Those at the top used intimidation to control behavior. Negativity ran rampant, leading to a 44% annual turnover rate.

If communication has historically been a problem, saying what you mean and doing what you say go a long way. After talking with his team and assessing the challenges the center faced, Ivan began creating the landscape for the changes to take place. By setting up committees, he involved most everyone at the comm center in enacting change.

One committee examined and revised standard operating procedures (SOPs), changed organizational charts, and wrote new policies. The Policy and Procedure Committee developed the SOPs and provided the future direction of the center from this level. Ivan reviewed the documentation, sent it to legal for minor edits, and then implemented it. Another committee was assigned the challenge of low morale; and as it happened, the Morale Committee was comprised of the most disgruntled people. Other supervisors and managers had written this group off, calling them "troublemakers." When assigned to the committee, however, their morale changed. They *owned* a part of the change process. They began to feel valued again.

Doing what you say is one part of inspiring trust—a part that People Driven Leaders do instinctively. They also understand that it's critical to entrust your team with true responsibility. I often hear line employees say, "It feels like management's hiring philosophy is 'just get warm butts in the seats.' We're trained to save lives, but it seems like we're disposable." The best 9-1-1 leaders involve as many people as possible in day-to-day operations. They delegate. They push decision-making power (and opportunity) down the line. They know that when you empower people, they feel valued. This can seem small, or inconsequential even. But to the employee, it can mean the difference between "just another day at the salt mine," and a rewarding a career.

In the midst of putting out daily fires, this can seem like a lot of work to the overwhelmed manager. However, it's much more work dealing with constant turnover, low morale, and all the headaches this brings.

At Polk County, Ivan was deeply invested in making the change effort a team endeavor. "Most in the comm center were involved in enacting change," Ivan said. As a result, things changed dramatically. With widespread employee buy-in, the daily tone improved. "People went from talking about how bad things were, to talking about positive changes and how they could further change things for the better."

In addition to a change in morale, there was an immediate decrease in overtime spending and sick time usage. The center saved $200,000 in overtime spending in the second year alone. Sick leave dropped by 54%. Turnover went from 44% to just 13% during the same timeframe.

With organizational trust, things once thought impossible are no longer so. It takes a certain kind of leader to do this. In Ivan's own words:

> Good leaders create a culture of quality assurance and accountability. Well-run dispatch centers are responsive, professional, and develop specific processes and procedures applied across the board. No one plays favorites or circumvents the culture's expectations.
>
> Morale directly impacts everything. If employees are unhappy, the public suffers. Poor morale leads to increased sick leave, unsatisfactory performance, turnover, and the inability to select in-house individuals for promotion. Good management establishes employee ownership, encourages potential, and nurtures individual strengths. A servant leader offsets challenges associated with stress and challenging work schedules. A self-serving leader has lost sight of priorities.

When there's trust, both from management and the line, mountains move. To maintain this momentum, the best leaders continually look for ways to empower the line.

Good management establishes employee ownership, encourages potential, and nurtures individual strengths. It makes some managers nervous to think that they can't do everything themselves. They aren't necessarily concerned about the amount of work they have to do but about delegating duties and giving away control. The type A perfectionist has a tendency to keep everything on her plate instead of risking a mistake made by a subordinate.

People Driven Leaders know they *can't* do everything alone, and it harms center culture to try. One center director gets feedback from his leadership team on everything from hiring, training, policy, and daily operations. This was a stark difference from the previous directors, who didn't share anything with line employees.

When a new director started involving others into the center's decision-making process, employees were initially apprehensive. Previous management had a habit of beating employees down, frequently doling out discipline without due process. "We were so scared of getting written up that we just kept our mouths shut," one supervisor explained. In time, employees began to trust the new director and to see that his intentions were true.

The new director's commitment to empowering the line translated into deeper commitment from these employees. As one said, "He empowered us to use our own minds and to think outside the box — we didn't need to be afraid anymore. This boosted our confidence and made room for us to do what we thought was required, instead of only doing what we were told." According to the employee, "This changed so much for me. I decided to commit to the organization. I wanted to see our center successful, happy and healthy. Now, as a supervisor, I try to empower people and to help them succeed. Their success is important to me." As the director empowered his team members, they, in turn, sought to empower those under their charge.

To empower your people, give clear guidance as to the expectations—guidance and vision—then free them to take chances. This type of leadership takes courage and trust, and it pays huge dividends.

Many ask, "What do leaders at the best centers *do* to create a workplace that people enjoy?" The person asking is almost always looking for specifics, like employee recognition programs, "bring your kids to work" days, handwritten notes, or birthday parties. These *can* help, don't get me wrong, but *what* these leaders do isn't the difference-maker. It's *who they are* and *why* they do it that is their secret sauce.

Every 9-1-1 professional is equipped with very special technology: a keen bullshit detector. A manager who is faking a genuine concern for their employees will be sniffed out in no time at all. The manager who isn't sincere—whose values are not in the best interest of the team—can use any and every morale improvement method, and it won't make a dent. A leader's actions must flow authentically from who they are.

When a leader authentically cares for and is truly people driven, employees feel like they know them. They know what to expect and are confident that their leader has their best interest at heart. What happens when we feel cared for, trusted and encouraged? We feel *safe*. We let our guard down. We can be vulnerable with each other. The best leaders in 9-1-1 are this way. They lead with vulnerability and create a feeling of safety.

In his book *Leaders Eat Last,* author Simon Sinek describes how being inside this "Circle of Safety" feels:

> It is easy to know when we are in the Circle of Safety because we can feel it. We feel valued by our colleagues and we feel cared for by our superiors. We become absolutely confident that the leaders of the organization and all those with whom we work are there for us and will do what they can to help us succeed. We become members of the group. We feel like we belong. When we believe that those inside our group,

those inside the Circle, will look out for us, it creates an environment or the free exchange of information and effective communication. This is fundamental to driving innovation, preventing problems from escalating and making organizations better equipped to defend themselves from the outside dangers and seize the opportunities.

Creating a feeling of safety doesn't stop with the manager or director. Every level of leadership at the center must aim to be this kind of leader, or the chain will break. It's helpful to know who the leaders in your organization are in order to understand who has the power to influence your center in such a way. Those in leadership roles are either making the center feel like a place where people *love working,* or a place where people would love to *quit working.*

Your center's formal leaders, outside of the highest levels of management, include training officers, lead dispatchers, operations managers, QA supervisors, tactical dispatchers, training coordinators, supervisors—anyone who has responsibility for directing specific organizational goals.

Then there are informal leaders. These individuals sometimes have more influence than formal leaders, especially during times of low morale and internal strife. Informal leaders are those who people choose to follow on their own. Absent strong, formal leadership, informal leaders will fill the void, as with certain centers' tenured folks. When there's entrenched and defiant informal leadership, it's even more important to have formal leaders who know what they're doing.

In some comm centers, the top of the organizational chart is a chief or a captain or a sheriff who has a large span of control. As a result, their focus is not necessarily on Communications, yet all decisions ultimately flow through this person. This tends to create a feeling of a void at the top and disconnection throughout Communications. In these situations, supervisors report wanting to do something to positively impact organizational life but feel powerless to do it. Others claim that while they've brought their concerns and solutions to the manager, nothing ever happens because that manager isn't empowered to take action. This can cause frustration and tank morale.

It's still possible to lead during these challenging times and for line supervisors at these centers to cultivate a feeling of safety, foster camaraderie, and take whatever action possible. The most important thing is not to lose hope. At one center, it took nearly nine years to get a bad manager reassigned from his post at the top of the Communications Division. During that time, the training coordinator stepped in as the informal leader to advocate for line staff. While unable to implement widespread change as she might've were she the manager, the training coordinator found she could buoy spirits and make her team feel valued nevertheless. She was the People Driven Leader at this center.

Self-Assessment

1. What can you give your people to own today?
2. Who are the informal leaders at your center who may threaten to derail your positive change initiative? This is another great topic of discussion for your supervisory team meetings.
3. How can you deploy these informal leaders to help instead of to hinder the initiative?
4. Which of The Five Key Characteristics are you strongest in? How does this impact your leadership ability?

THE FIVE KEY CHARACTERISTICS OF A PEOPLE DRIVEN LEADER

1. Exhibiting emotional intelligence
2. Inspiring values, or knowing what you stand for
3. An ability to set the bar and articulate clear expectations
4. A commitment to excellence, or continual improvement
5. The ability to inspire trust

CHAPTER 4

BE THE TYPE OF LEADER YOU'D WANT TO FOLLOW

Since leadership is an inside job, there is much you can do to improve your leadership ability and to become more like the leaders I describe in this book. In fact, not one of the exemplary leaders I talk about were born this way. They learned by watching, reading, talking with other leaders, and then practicing their way over time. They engaged in some or all of the following:

Classes

Ask your training coordinator about upcoming training class offerings, both classroom and online. LinkedIn has a whole series of online video modules that can help you improve.

Conferences

APCO, NENA and IAED national conferences are chock-full of leadership instruction tracks, where you can get inspiration, tactics and approaches. APCO and NENA state conferences are a great local option.

Books

They say that "leaders are readers," and picking up a great leadership book can open your eyes to a new perspective. In the last chapter, I mentioned *Leaders Eat Last*, by Simon Sinek (anything by Simon is amazing), and *Emotional Intelligence 2.0* by Travis Bradbury and Jean Greaves. More of my favorite leadership books are named in the *Suggestions for Additional Reading* section in the back of the book.

Mentorship

Emulating the best leaders can rub off. The best mentoring relationship is one where you meet with your mentor on a regular basis. Many who work in a communications center are in their first job. They haven't necessarily taken leadership or management courses, and they need guidance.

Seminars

There are a host of leadership seminars outside of the 9-1-1 industry where you can learn leadership principles from both a personal and organizational perspective. The International Association of Chiefs of Police (IACP) offer training opportunities; additionally, your local college, and even your police training academy, can point you in the right direction.

It might sound like there's a lot to do, but becoming a better leader is as simple and straightforward as being the type of boss *you* would want. Think back to the best manager or supervisor you've had in your career. What are some of that person's qualities? What did they do differently from your other not-so-great bosses? Were they positive? Encouraging? Approachable? Knowledgeable?

The consistent thread running through each conversation I've had with the best 9-1-1 center leaders is their willingness to put themselves in their subordinates' places. They walk the floor. They work a console when needed. They are present and available. They are servants to those under their charge.

Self-Assessment

1. Identify a training opportunity that can help you improve your leadership ability. When can you schedule yourself to go?
2. What area of improvement is the most important for you to focus on?

PEOPLE DRIVEN LEADER PROFILE

Chad Chewning, Director at Livingston County 9-1-1 Central Dispatch in Howell, Michigan, is this type of leader. Mentored in servant leadership since early in his career, Chad was brought up under the philosophy that "my way is not always the correct way." His approach served him well. He was promoted to Captain of his fire company by age 26, worked as a center manager for American Medical Response for 18 years, and then spent several years in Communications at Oakland County Sheriff's Office before hiring on at Livingston County. Chad's leadership style was just what Livingston County 9-1-1 Central Dispatch needed.

When Chad started at Livingston, things weren't going well. By most metrics, the center was failing. Morale had been low for years. The staff was completely resigned to the situation, burned-out, and numb, and they had been overlooked by previous management. The overtime was non-stop as a skeleton crew of 14 employees did the work of 24. Hiring efforts were zero-sum for a few reasons, all of which came back to management.

There was no nationally recognized training program. Training policies were completely subjective; you passed if they liked you. Dispatch center management was also in charge of hiring. After a 12-hour sit-along, the two shifts—days and nights—got to vote for whom they liked. With no real objectivity or standards, this method did not work. The year before Chad joined the agency, 37 trainees failed out of the program. Years of neglect, lack of oversight, and a generally hands-off approach by management up to this point insured that this norm would continue unless the county 9-1-1 board did something differently.

They looked outside the organization for a deputy director who could make a positive difference. After a search that netted 42 applicants, Chad was hired.

From the beginning, Chad was very clear about where the organization needed to be, but he was open to the specific path the team would take to get there. After just three days on the job, Chad moved in the direction of his vision. He sat down with everyone and gave them an opportunity to speak, bridging the divide the tough years had created. He was particularly detailed about his expectations with supervisors. He explained to this group that they either needed to be on board with the changes, or not. If not, "You might not be right for the job," he suggested. Two of the three supervisors agreed and left.

With the help of a reinvigorated supervisory team, Chad made sweeping changes to outdated policies and procedures, created a certified training officer (CTO) program (employees previously had not received any training), and did whatever possible to build rapport. It didn't take long for staff to see that the new director walked his talk. He was there for them, provided clear guidance, and then let them figure things out. Chad said, "Sure, I'm the boss, but I work for you."

The biggest task Chad faced was building rapport with staff and rekindling trust in management. Only 8 weeks into his new role, Chad and his leadership team began converting policies and procedures to align with this aim. Past practice was for officers to control what call they went out on. Within six weeks, the policy was switched to direct dispatch. A 22-page manual previously explained how to dispatch an ambulance. Chad went to EMS and said, "You have two pages for this procedure," and they did it.

CTO training was brought in, and all instructors went through the program. Prior to this, CTOs had received no training. Employees received uniforms, improving team camaraderie. The interview process was next. The hokey ways of subjective voting were out. Chad introduced a three-phase process, including a psychological exam and CritiCall screening in Phase 1; a first interview with a supervisor, a CTO, and a shift leader as Phase 2; and a second interview with Chad (director), the HR director, and the operations manager as Phase 3. County HR led the process, greatly improving objectivity and thereby the quality of candidates.

It didn't take long for the staff to see that Chad was there for them. He did what he said he was going to do. In the words of one supervisor during that time, "After talking with him, we were hopeful. We agreed to give him a chance and to see what would happen." An amazing turnaround in morale resulted as the staff saw they were getting the support they'd never had before. Within one year of these changes, a center that couldn't meet minimum staffing was now fully staffed. The 9-1-1 board said, "If you get fully staffed [at 24 positions], we'll give you more bodies." They followed through, plus let Chad hire four operations managers.

In addition to operational changes, Chad invested in his staff in another way. He bought all new equipment—consoles, radios, monitors, CAD system, chairs—and renovated the dispatch center. Before the equipment upgrade and renovation, the center had been left unchanged since its formation in 1999. Chad was hired into a center with paint flaking off the walls and equipment obviously worn-out after 15 years of continuous use. He immediately changed this.

In effect, Chad helped his people realize their fullest potential. He didn't fire everyone and start over. He didn't bring in a bunch of outsiders to do the jobs of the existing team members. Instead, he said, in very clear terms, "Here's where we need to go; let's get there together." A People Driven Leader trusts his people to know the way. The existing personnel at Livingston County 9-1-1 Central Dispatch were dedicated. They loved the job. They wanted each other to succeed. And when they were given the right tools, they did.

"Chad inspired commitment to the organization," said a tenured supervisor, "not commitment to him. In fact, Chad will never take credit for what's happened."

In my conversations with Chad, I'm struck by his deep humility. He always pays deference to his team. I caught up with Chad once at a conference and said, "I'd love to hear how things are going at the center since our last conversation; do you have a few minutes?"

Without hesitation, he said, "Oh, you should really talk to the Ops Manager; she's done such a great job."

A People Driven Leader is a facilitator for the organization's growth. By using the resources at his disposal, Chad enabled his team to perform at a higher level than ever before. He shared his vision, set expectations, and then stepped aside. This type of leadership creates more leaders. It unifies the team around a common purpose. It helps people understand their true worth.

In Chad's words: "The highest leaders must be physically present and seen. The staff need to know your face, not your rank. People *have* to respect your rank; but if they don't respect you as a person, you'll get nothing done. You need to meet with your team and when you walk in there, there's no rank. They know who you are. You must be willing to sit next to your people, ask them what their job is, and then ask, 'How can we make things better?' And then really listen to what's offered."

WHAT THE 9-1-1 INDUSTRY SAYS ABOUT PEOPLE DRIVEN LEADERSHIP

Using the research and standards produced by the 9-1-1 industry trade associations, it's easy to see what is already known about People Driven Leadership. The results of Project RETAINS and its follow-ups point directly to the importance of prioritizing people.

In addition to Project RETAINS, several APCO and NENA professional standards highlight specific elements of the people side of the business. The professional standards offered by these trade associations are designed as *minimum* training standards and core competencies for communications center managers, directors, supervisors, training coordinators, and more. Since our focus is on People Driven Leadership, we'll focus here on the standards for supervisors and managers/directors.

In 2012, APCO Standards Development Committee released the *Core Competencies and Minimum Training Standards for Public Safety Communications Supervisor*. This standard identifies the core competencies and minimum training requirements for public safety communications supervisors. According to the standard, "this position provides leadership and guidance to employees in order to achieve the Agency's mission, while providing service to the public and the Agency's responders."

The standard clearly lays out the core competencies and minimum training standards at both the agency level, and the individual supervisor level. It's very detailed and offers some eye-opening "minimum qualifications" that deal specifically with emotional intelligence. A section on professional competence states, "The Supervisor shall demonstrate team leadership concepts, including being an effective team member, as well as developing and managing high-performing teams. The Supervisor shall demonstrate the ability to communicate with superiors, peers, and subordinates in a positive and constructive manner."

It's recommended that at a minimum, supervisors know how to effectively build and lead high-performing teams. This means they must know what both team leadership and a high-performing team look like. They must be excellent communicators, but also do so with positivity while fostering team camaraderie (instead of tearing people down).

In 2014, APCO released their *Core Competencies and Minimum Training Standards for Public Safety Communications Manager / Director*. Not surprisingly, the standard holds that People Driven Leadership is the *minimum* standard, not merely the exception to the rule. According to the standard, "The position [of Manager/Director] is typically tasked with managing and directing all aspects of a public safety communications center, while effectively utilizing leadership skills, resources, and partnerships in order to successfully provide emergency communications service."

The very beginning of the standard, in the section called "Organizational Integrity," states, "The Manager/Director shall foster and create effective working relationships with all personnel within the organization and with individuals and organizations external to the Agency. The Manager/Director shall encourage and support the highest quality of workplace team interaction and behavior."

So, at the minimum, a communications manager/director must know what effective working relationships look like, and then they must be able to create them—not only inside their organization, but with external stakeholders as well. They must also be encouraging, supportive and an emotionally intelligent person who knows what high quality team interaction and behavior looks like and feels like, so they can instill it in their organization.

While the majority of each standard addresses individual training and competencies, they also outline the agency's responsibilities for providing training to both new and veteran supervisors in accordance with this standard. "The Agency shall establish no less than these minimum training requirements while complying with all local, state, federal, and tribal laws. The Agency shall define the baseline qualifications in addition to requisite cognitive, affective, and psychomotor skills needed to achieve compliance with this standard."

If the 9-1-1 industry has collectively determined, through convening committees and years-long discussions (both of which are required to produce an industry standard), that the *people* dimension is of vital importance—then where is the opportunity to bring more of it into comm center life? If those appointed to leadership positions within your center follows a long line of technicians, they are likely hiring more technicians. The questions that technicians ask in interviews are geared to quantify technical skills, not people skills. Changing your interview to focus on people-oriented values can help.

None of this stuff is easy. And the above examples are just one section from each of the standards. There's a ton more. It's no wonder that technicians would rather focus on the radios and equipment. This "people stuff" is scary! It's also no wonder the best leaders have followed in the footsteps of other great leaders. They've been mentored in People Driven Leadership. They've been shown the way.

THE SIGNS OF A PEOPLE DRIVEN CENTER

The following eleven areas define the components of the people side of the business, and each require People Driven Leadership. We'll use the example set by Livingston County 9-1-1 Central Dispatch [from the People Driven Leader Profile, beginning on page 55]:

1. Communication

A People Driven Center embraces free-flowing communication across all ranks. Communication is frequent amongst line employees, as well as between the line and supervision. The communication must be two-way and non-threatening. It doesn't consist merely of the gossip mill. Face-to-face discussion, in addition to written documentation, is important.

For years, the staff at Livingston County 9-1-1 Central Dispatch never felt heard. They had resigned themselves to feeling like the "forgotten stepchildren." Within days of the new director's arrival, this changed. He walked the comm center floor and invited his employees to sit down and share their challenges. He also used this time to explain where he was coming from and to emphasize that he was on their side. Without hesitation, the new director, Chad, gave team members his attention, heard them out, and then shared the vision forward.

2. Participation and Involvement

A People Driven Center is inspired when all levels of the organization are appropriately involved in decision-making. Employees possess organizational ownership when they feel as though they have a hand in improvements. The organization must reflect a sense of openness. Fear and intimidation are not components of the cultural landscape.

According to a supervisor who worked at Livingston County for years before and after the new director's arrival, the old management team was always disciplining employees. "Everyone was in trouble, no matter what," she explained. The dominant management style was to use force and fear. The new director changed that. "We were given guidance as to the expectations, guidance and vision, and then [we were] freed to take chances."

3. Loyalty and Commitment

An atmosphere of high interpersonal trust exists in a People Driven Center. Employees generally feel proud to tell people where they work and what they do. They look forward to coming to work and feel their center is a good place to work. They willingly attend work-related meetings.

Without trust, there is no loyalty or commitment. Because Chad showed his staff he cared about and supported them—by making the changes he said he would, and by empowering staff to take an active role in rebuilding the organization—their commitment was refreshed.

4. Morale

Positive morale is critical to a healthy climate. This is demonstrated by a friendly atmosphere where employees like each other, like their jobs, and approach their jobs with enthusiasm. Overall, employees are motivated both personally and on behalf of the organization.

As communication flowed throughout Livingston County 9-1-1, inspiring participation and awakening loyalty, improved morale was a natural result. Who wouldn't want to work at a center where you feel like your efforts are recognized and rewarded?

5. Institutional Reputation

A People Driven Center takes pride in the perception of a positive reputation. Employees and managers share involvement in improving relationships with the external community (e.g., citizens, surrounding agencies, officers, community organizations). The center enjoys a respectable reputation both externally and within the department. Employees, in general, value the reputation of where they work.

Consistently the lowest-rated center in the state before this transition, the staff dreaded coming to work and surely didn't speak highly of their workplace. Only a year into implementation of this positive change initiative, a dramatic change had taken place. The word got out not only across the state, but across the country.

Before the transition, applicants who were asked the question, "Why do you want to work here?" would respond with things like, "Because I want to be close to family, and I need a job."

After the transition, applicants responded, "Because you're accredited, because you're the best. I want to work for the best."

People from all over the country apply at Livingston County because people are always looking for a 9-1-1 center worth working for. In one instance, a 19-year veteran of dispatch left her former center and moved across the state after accepting her job here.

6. Ethics

In general, unethical behavior does not exist in a People Driven Center. A positive ethical climate can be facilitated by an employee-driven code of ethics for the center. In places like these, employees tend to value character and see no place for politics at work.

In addition to generally ignoring the staff, the old directors at Livingston County spent the funds allocated specifically for 9-1-1 on surrounding patrol divisions. They were retired police officers and didn't see any problem with it. They blamed the repugnant working conditions on the 9-1-1 board, saying, "My hands are tied, sorry. Funding is the way it is because we have to prioritize FD and PD."

When Chad found the old directors had been directing 9-1-1 funds to field responders in the form of new equipment, he immediately corrected it. The next time the Sheriff came asking for money, Chad simply said, "Sorry, you'll have to find your own."

7. Performance Recognition

Employees are encouraged and supported to reach their full potential. In general, they feel valued and appreciated. They are appropriately recognized for achievement within a climate of appreciation and caring.

Before, no one at Livingston received recognition for anything. Following the transition, they implemented a QA program and used it. High scorers were invited to attend state and national conferences, go to board meetings, and attend county-level government meetings.

8. Goal Alignment

Within a healthy climate, organizational goals are usually achieved. The relationship between goals, individual roles and team roles is clear. Workers can identify the overall focus of their assignment; they have appropriately participated in goal setting and can readily identify goals within the organization.

Prior to the transition, the center didn't have goals outside of "get through the day." There was no inspiration, no vision. Chad changed that by sharing his goals for where the center needed to be and by getting everyone on board with the mission.

9. Leadership

Leadership relationships play an important role in a People Driven Center. Employees must perceive leaders as working well within and throughout the organization. Leaders must be seen as acting in the best interest of the department and as generally friendly and approachable.

Every change at Livingston County was made possible by a specific type of leadership. Without it, it would've been more of the same old.

10. Training & Development

Considering the many options available for employment today, employee development is a must. A healthy environment is often due partly to the level of support for training and development existing in the organization. Formal succession planning must be facilitated, and employees must participate in this process.

Prior to 2014, employees at Livingston County 9-1-1 received no additional training outside of new employee training, and even this program wasn't objective. Trainees passed if the instructor liked them. Employee weren't allowed to go to additional training, even though the funds were allocated.

Chad changed this immediately. He instituted a coaching and mentoring program, sent employees to outside training classes and conferences, and let them see they were a part of the larger 9-1-1 community. He told his supervisors, "You are training your replacement. You must take time to mentor the staff."

11. Resource Utilization

The appropriate use of organization resources is another critical component of a healthy culture. Employees must perceive resources are shared appropriately and fairly, and in a manner consistent with expectations for achievement.

Many underfunded and generally neglected centers are forced to make do with the bare minimum. Other centers fall under the purview of a larger agency whose administrators have never gone to bat for their communications section, or who simply don't know of a better way. There may be resources available to change things, but they have left these options unearthed.

Only by assessing your employees' perceptions of each of these areas can we begin to understand where improvement is possible and necessary. Some center managers may shy away from taking a closer look at the people-side because they fear what they might find. Others may not know where to start. Sussing out deep issues in an effort to make lasting positive changes is a sign of strength and commitment. Since the changes will likely take some time and effort to achieve, it's also a sign of courage.

Self-Assessment

1. Which of the eleven areas above are showing you signs that something needs to change at your center?
2. What action can you take this week to address this area of deficiency? Once you've addressed the most glaring challenge, go to the next one.

CHAPTER 5
CULTURE AND CLIMATE: HOW AND WHY THE SOFT STUFF MATTERS

All the organizational variables and individual characteristics (or lack thereof) described in the previous chapters come together to create the culture and climate of the center. An organization's culture is typically viewed as those deeply held values, beliefs, assumptions, symbols, and rituals shared across the organization. According to the *Harvard Business Review*, "Organizational culture is the sum of the values and rituals which serve as 'glue' to integrate the members of the organization." Culture describes the social context of an organization's workplace.

When a culture is at its best, it will energize employees and make them feel good about coming into work. At its worst, it can drag down productivity and undermine long-term success.

An organization's culture is shared among all or most of the workforce as a result of lengthy periods of repetition and indoctrination. It's also reinforced through a socialization process from the center's leaders to new employees.

Because organizational culture is so deeply ingrained and takes a relatively long time to become established, it can also take a while to change. Add to this the fact that very few people are open to or like to change, and you've got resting inertia holding things in a stuck place. To stimulate a transformation in culture, the behaviors and mindsets that led to its formation must also change.

CLIMATE

A center's **climate** represents those behaviors, attitudes, and feelings that reflect the day-to-day operations across the organization. Climate describes the psychological impacts of the workplace; it emphasizes the shared perception of how things are done.

Think of organizational climate in terms of relationships and the human side of things. Compared to an organization's culture, an organization's climate is less ingrained and usually easier to change; it is more malleable and influential in the short-term.

Therefore, if center leadership is interested in making improvements in a relatively short period of time, then focusing on the organization's climate is one approach that could help. By understanding an organization's climate, managers are better able to understand the fundamental perceptions, feelings, and attitudes that drive center performance. As a result of this increased understanding, an organization stands to gain improved productivity from one of its most valuable resources: its people.

Understanding your center's perceptions, feelings and attitudes requires being in tune with these things. This is the realm of emotional intelligence. Without EQ, it's nearly impossible to clearly see why the culture is as it is, and it's even more difficult to improve it. Culture and climate work together to influence how employees feel about coming into work. It's not possible to have a high-performance center without a culture that promotes it. Likewise, if the daily climate is overwhelmingly negative, it's likely that the culture of your organization is promoting this.

Quick actions that immediately illustrate the potential for positive change can shift the climate from deeply negative and cynical to somewhat optimistic, thereby fostering more engagement. The very cynical employees are on the "actively disengaged" part of the spectrum of employee engagement (see diagram on the next page), at the very bottom. A glimmer of optimism can open an opportunity that was closed long before, converting even the Negative Nelly's into contributing partners to the change initiative.

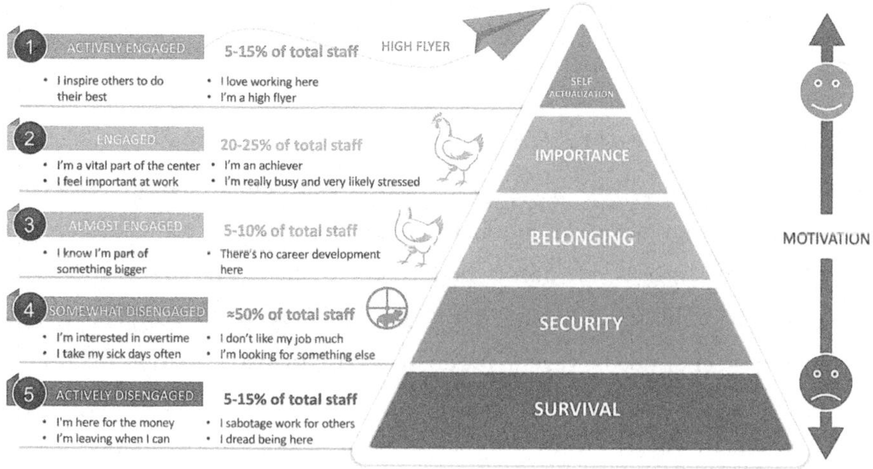

Some of the quick-action initiatives deployed by the People Driven Leaders studied here included:

1. Sitting down with every employee, one-on-one, to ask about their perceptions of the workplace and why they believe things are this way.

2. Locating the resources and spending money on issues screaming for attention (dilapidated consoles, paint flaking off the walls of the center, broken chairs).

3. Inviting employees into the culture-change conversation in a meaningful way, including designated committees, weekly meetings, or face-to-face exchanges.

4. Soliciting feedback on the "hot button" issues and moving quickly to alleviate the pressure they cause (uniforms, shift rotations, CAD adjustments).

These seemingly small efforts go a long way in proving that People Driven Leaders are walking their talk. This is where they lay the building blocks of trust. Inviting the entire team (or, with larger centers, a change management team designated by peers) into a planning session where they are invited to brainstorm issues that, with support and attention, could shift within the next four to twelve weeks and move the dial considerably. If nothing else, the early initiatives work to temporarily retain good people who are thinking about resigning.

A shift in the climate makes employees more willing to embrace the deeper changes required to change *culture*, which is the ultimate goal. One of the challenges with culture is that, if leadership is not intentional about shaping it, the organization may unintentionally adopt a mindset and habits that are not conducive to success. I don't believe that managers and supervisors intentionally drive people out of the job, but by perpetually neglecting employees' deeper needs, certain perceptions are formed ("we don't matter"), and this defines the culture over time. Because it's subtle and nuanced, people issues like these can feel frustrating or even a waste of time to address. "Who has the time?" we may think. "There are fires to put out!"

Based on my research, however, these things matter more than anything. To put it simply, you can't afford to ignore how people feel about working at your center. If you aren't intentionally creating a positive place to work, you are unintentionally creating the opposite.

CULTURE EATS STRATEGY FOR BREAKFAST

Failing to address culture will derail any center's plans for success. This is why so many attempts at getting to "fully staffed" fail. Everywhere you turn, there's another article or study or webinar about staffing challenges in 9-1-1. The stress of the job is often cited as the primary reason why people leave, but when we look deeper, it's clear there's more to the story. If the nature of the job was the primary reason that people don't stay in the profession, then we wouldn't see *any* centers able to keep staff. This isn't the case.

If this weren't evidence enough that the stress of the job has only a limited impact on retention, recent research provides further proof. In several studies involving 9-1-1 telecommunicators, eight of the top ten stressors have nothing to do with the work itself. Those who are sitting under the headset state they're more stressed by internal challenges like poor leadership, management/administration, aging equipment, lack of recognition, and feeling like Communications is the overlooked cog in the machine of the larger department.

Claiming that the stress of 9-1-1 work is why we can't keep our comm centers staffed sounds like a plausible story. And yes, the work *can* be stressful, but it's not the biggest challenge for those in the job. In fact, it isn't even *the second or third* biggest challenge. Blaming the inherent nature of the work for why people leave leads to a problem: center managers who believe this are less apt to address the real problems that are driving great candidates out the door.

Blaming the work also limits the actions available to address the problem. If we view "the work" as the problem, the only solution is to find more people. And it's a viable option if the comm center is in an area with a large applicant pool. The centers experiencing the most challenges, however, are in small communities where they've already exhausted the applicant pool.

"Just hire more people" isn't the best option for anyone, really. Centers in large communities may subscribe to this, but it's mostly because they haven't quantified the true cost of all that recruitment, hiring, and training. And eventually, they will also run out of qualified applicants.

Or, as we're beginning to see, people in some communities simply are not interested in a career in 9-1-1. Maybe they've heard about the challenges. Perhaps they don't understand the profession well enough to jump into it. Whatever the case is, if fewer and fewer are submitting applications, then it's more important than ever to keep those that are hired.

Building a People Driven Center staffed with People Driven Leaders is the way to hire them and keep them.

Self-Assessment

1. Would you rate the climate and culture of your center as positive or negative?
2. How is this perception of culture reflected in your employees' behavior?
3. What daily behaviors need to change in order for the culture to change?
4. What must you (and others) do to change these behaviors?

CHAPTER 6
ASSESSING WHETHER YOUR CENTER IS PEOPLE ORIENTED

Now that we have a better understanding of what we mean when we discuss the overall "health" of a center, we can begin understanding how people driven your center is by performing the quick assessment below. An even better idea is to have some of your employees complete the assessment and see what you discover.

ASSESS THE "PEOPLE ORIENTATION" OF YOUR CENTER:	Yes	or No
1. Frequent communication between supervisors and employees is encouraged.	1	0
2. Open communication exists between managerial levels.	1	0
3. Employees are appropriately involved in decision making.	1	0
4. Employees are proud to tell people where they work.	1	0
5. An atmosphere of high interpersonal trust exists.	1	0
6. High morale exists in the organization.	1	0
7. Employees are motivated.	1	0
8. A friendly atmosphere exists in the organization.	1	0
9. The organization has a respectable reputation.	1	0
10. Employees value the organization's reputation.	1	0
11. Employees act ethically.	1	0
12. A written code of conduct exists and is followed.	1	0
13. Employees feel valued and appreciated by supervision and by each other.	1	0
14. Appropriate recognition for achievement is common.	1	0

15. Organizational goals are usually achieved. 1 0
16. Employees can identify organizational goals. 1 0
17. Supervisors act in the best interest of the organization. 1 0
18. Supervisors are friendly and approachable. 1 0
19. A budget exists for training and development, and it's used. 1 0
20. Resources are shared fairly across the organization. 1 0

Total Points:

SCORING: THE "PEOPLE ORIENTATION" OF YOUR CENTER

17 - 20 points	Positively to fairly positively oriented towards your people	Continue being proactive. Consider cutting out some of the bureaucracy and barriers to communication. Recommendations: use proactive measures; utilize training and development programs; engage in innovation.
13 - 16 points	Your people may be feeling overlooked or undervalued	More of the above, but do it sooner - no procrastination! Things could fall apart quickly; put immediate effort into improving conditions. Reevaluate training programs, update recognition/evaluation procedures, and create and share a code of conduct. Use benchmarking to compare with leaders in the industry.
9 - 12 points	"Is anyone there?" Your people are convinced they don't matter and are likely looking elsewhere	Find out exactly where the problems are. In other words, rework the organizational structure. Where you can't remove barriers, create alternative pathways. You may need to change hiring practices, consider changes in management, and align the vision and practice of the organization.
5 - 8 points	Your people feel like they have no other options, so they stay	Your center is likely barely surviving. The job gets done, but only the very minimum. You need to consider extreme options before a member of the community your agency serves dies.
0 - 4 points	It's surprising your center has any employees	Charge the paddles! There is low probability that you can breathe life back into the organization. There is a very slim chance that employees will continue to work with this organization.

Exercise Debrief

What did you learn about your center's people orientation in this exercise?

The interesting thing about this exercise—which was adapted from the private sector for 9-1-1—is that if a private organization were facing "death," this company would quickly go out of business if they failed to take drastic action. In 9-1-1, however, the work must still get done, and it does. Line employees and supervisors who really want to help people and to make a difference are forced to do more with less. With funding coming from public resources, many communications centers are very poorly run, wasting thousands on overtime and poor hiring practices. They aren't ever going to go out of business, so it can seem like there's no real reason to look at the underlying issues.

What my team usually discovers when we undergo a center assessment is that *all* centers have some area that needs improvement. In particular, almost every center can benefit from forming a clear vision and a set of values, and that's what we'll cover in the next section.

PART TWO:

TRANSFORMATION

CHAPTER 7

VISION: WE'RE LOST WITHOUT IT

There are two stonemasons building a wall. You walk up to the first stonemason and ask, "Do you like your job?" He looks up at you and replies, "I've been building this wall for as long as I can remember. The work is monotonous. I work in the scorching hot sun all day. The stones are heavy, and lifting them day after day can be backbreaking. I'm not even sure if this project will be completed in my lifetime. But it's a job. It pays the bills." You thank him for his time and walk on.

About thirty feet away, you walk up to a second stonemason. You ask him the same question, "Do you like your job?" He looks up and replies, "I l love my job. I'm building a cathedral. Sure, I've been working on this wall for as long as I can remember, and yes, the work is sometimes monotonous. I work in the scorching hot sun all day. The stones are heavy, and lifting them day after day can be backbreaking. I'm not even sure if this project will be completed in my lifetime. But I'm building a cathedral."

The work is the same, yet the two stonemasons have very different views. When the stonemason who is *just building a wall* gets up in the morning, he likely dreads going to work. While at work, he probably drags his feet, complains to his coworkers, and hems and haws about how "no one cares around here anyway" as he does just enough to keep from getting in trouble, and then he shuffles home. His home life is impacted too, with his negative attitude in full force while sitting at the dinner table, griping to his wife and children. This negativity impacts his health as well, sapping his drive to stay active and to eat well.

The stonemason building a cathedral is passionate about the difference he is making. It isn't an *overly* optimistic view. He doesn't deny the hardships of the scorching sun, the backbreaking work or the possibility of never seeing completion. To him, these are undeniable aspects of the job—all part of his opportunity to build something worth building. His passion likely overflows into his personal life as well. He leaves work tired from the hard day, but there's still a bounce in his step. Because he finds his work meaningful, his life has meaning. In fact, his job may represent just one of the reflections of his meaningful life. With something to live for, one lives in a much different way.

This is the catalyzing power of a clear vision. The stonemason who doesn't like his job is focused only on the task at hand, which is backbreaking, monotonous and boring. This is all he can see, and this limited view also hinders his ability to derive meaning from the work. The stonemason who loves his job knows *why* he comes to work each day. He's building something grand. He's driven by his why, and it pushes him beyond the limitations posed by the more challenging aspects of the job.

It's tempting to look at this example and place blame or responsibility on the individual. We might say, "Some employees are positive, some are negative. There's nothing we can do about that." Much like saying, "This is a nationwide problem, not just a local problem," regarding staffing and retention. If you believe there's nothing you can do about them, you're less apt to take bold and decisive action to solve persistent organizational problems that continually tug at morale.

Fortunately, the research is hopeful and conclusive. It tells us that employee engagement matters—*a lot*. And leaders who prioritize the aspects of organizational life that enhance employee engagement foster higher levels of employee satisfaction and overall performance.

To engage employees at a high level, the best centers start with an integrating vision and a humanizing mission. Vision and mission give the organization purpose, something for the team to rally around. Without a collective understanding of where the organization is headed and why, employees feel disconnected and adrift, victim to the hardships of organizational realities outside their control. Without a clear mission (like building a cathedral), telling your employees, "Get on board!" may rightfully prompt the response, "Get on board with what? We've received no direction!" A directionless crew is just going through the motions, collecting paychecks and waiting for retirement.

STEPPING FORWARD

In 2009, Grand Junction Regional Emergency Communications Center had reached a breaking point. Nearly 75% of trainees were leaving the center before completing the training program. Overall turnover was 35%. Mandatory OT and excessive sick time usage were the norm. Exit interviews told a horrible tale of bullying and mistreatment, from both trainees and line employees.

Unwilling to accept this as the norm, the center's manager and assistant manager decided something had to change. With the help of a consultant, they began to ask important questions about the center's future. The most important of these questions was, "How do we want to treat people?" The amazing changes that followed were the result of hearing, loud and clear, how every team member answered this question.

The answers were crystallized in the center's newly minted Mission & Values Statement:

We protect those who serve,
we serve those who protect,
we help those in need.
Anytime and every time.

We will achieve these goals and provide excellent customer service by adhering to these values:

Integrity, Teamwork & Respect.

Rather than a pithy corporate slogan that merely looks good but doesn't result in action, this center's statement became the path forward. Every team member had a part in creating it. Because they were all unanimously bought into it, the values formed the foundation for hiring, training, daily operations, discipline, and termination.

In addition to creating an organizational culture based in strong values, center leadership set a concrete goal of becoming the best center in Colorado by a certain date. Through the efforts of the entire team, this vision became a reality: Grand Junction Regional Emergency Communications Center was named Colorado NENA/APCO Communication Center of the Year. This was no small feat for a center that just two years earlier struggled to attract, train and keep top talent.

Self-Assessment

1. Does your Communications division have a dedicated mission statement, separate from the larger agency it's a part of (if applicable)?
2. If so, do your people know what this mission represents and how it affects their work on a daily basis?
3. If not, what methods do you use to unify your team?

If you don't have a vision or mission for your center, this is a great opportunity to assign a sense of real identity to your center and let your people get involved in the process of pronouncing what you stand for. In the next chapter, you'll be given the opportunity to create your own vision.

THE PROCESS OF UNDERSTANDING YOUR CENTER'S VISION

The difference between a People Driven Center and the rest is striking—both in terms of productivity levels, and the way it feels to work in them. It may seem trivial to focus so much on a mission statement, but the mission statement in this case is actually an embodiment of the center's vision. That's why it's so important to answer the following six questions, for your employees and the organization as a whole. The answers to these questions form the foundation for a vision of success. They offer clarity around what the center stands for, the kind of employee who is the right fit, and how teams should complete their daily work.

The six questions are:

1. Why do we exist?
2. How do we behave?
3. What do we do?
4. How will we succeed?
5. What is the most important, right now?
6. Who must do what?

Communications center leadership should be responsible for crafting your center's vision, while involving as many others in the organization as possible. In fact, the more employees who are part of in this creative endeavor, the better. One large center, with over 100 full-time employees, put together a Mission and Vision Committee of employees nominated by their peers. Another agency had a small group do the initial brainstorming and invited anyone else who was interested to participate in refining it.

A word of advice: your initial request for volunteers may fall on deaf ears. Employees who have felt overlooked for years may not trust the newfound good intentions management is expressing. One way to overcome this is to reach out directly to those who might be a good fit for the project and to encourage them to be a part of the solution moving forward. If the status quo no longer works for the majority, speak to the promise of a better future and how this unified mission will help make it a reality.

Some communications center leaders believe that the mission, purpose or vision of the larger agency they are a part of (Sheriff's Office, County Police, City PD, etc.) serves well enough. This may be the case for some centers, but in nearly every center I've visited, I've seen a couple things: a) no one actually *knows* the larger agency's mission statement, and b) if they *do* know it, employees have no idea how it applies to their daily work life. Unfortunately, without a unifying mission, it's very difficult to bring a team of type A over-achievers together to accomplish a common goal.

Even if you opt to use the mission and vision of your larger agency, chances are good that it doesn't resonate as deeply as one created by the comm center staff would. The business of 9-1-1 communications is unique and requires its own description, in terms related to the work done. Police, fire and EMS work done in the field is different than the work done inside the walls of the comm center. Your center's vision and mission must reflect this uniqueness, unapologetically. As Monica Million, former Ops Manager at Grand Junction Regional Communications Center, pointed out, "Our mission may not be the same as the rest of the department or agency, and that's ok."

Let's take another look at Grand Junction RECC's Vision Statement for a great example of what we're talking about. The entire document includes their Purpose, Mission, and Values, which work with and inform each other. Here they all are:

Purpose

We protect those who serve,
We serve those who protect,
We help those in need.
Anytime and every time.

Mission

Answer	We answer the call for those in need, gathering critical information.
Send	We send the appropriate assistance as quickly as we can.
Assist	We assist responders while giving life-saving instruction to those in need.
Protect	We protect our citizens and responders through vigilance and accurate recording of location and actions taken.

Values

We will achieve these goals and provide excellent customer service by adhering to these values:

Integrity Teamwork Respect

The best vision statements provide guidance during challenging times: while on the phone with an irate caller; working a critical incident; interacting with your team members when the shit is hitting the fan. Employees should be able to quickly recollect what the center stands for and how they should respond.

A powerful vision works both ways. Employees will know how to behave and what will be tolerated, and they can also know if they agree with it. A clear vision statement empowers team members at every level of the organization. Supervisors don't have to grasp in the dark when it comes to sticky personnel challenges. Employees don't have to wonder if they're doing the right thing.

Let's take a look at the six questions posed at the beginning of the chapter in more detail along with examples of centers who've applied them.

Why Do We Exist?

Employees in your organization, at every level, need to know that at the heart of what they do lies something grand and aspirational: saving lives;

helping the community; being the one who answers the call. These reasons all breathe life into the daily grind.

The first question calls out the center's purpose and reason for existing. When center leadership sits down and decides why they come into work each day, this singular purpose can unite the most disparate group. It offers the organization a common language to describe what you all do as a team.

A good place to focus for this answer is to consider who the work of the center is impacting. Looking at the purpose statement above, it's clear Grand Junction views their primary reason for existing as threefold: to protect first responders, to serve their first responders, and to help those in need. Reading the statement, faces pop into mind of those whose lives the center affects: police, fire, EMS and the community.

Making the community a better place with each contact is an inspirational vision. Seeing in your mind the face of the first responder you're helping or the family member your CPR instructions have saved humanizes the work. Explicitly stating this as your purpose has the same effect. Daily actions aligned with an inspirational purpose feel more important because they are.

How Do We Behave?

"You become what you tolerate," one director said to me as she described her passion for bringing her center's values to life. She went on to tell me that her center had not been known for its successes in the past. Trainee washout was over 50%, annual turnover nearly 40%. These metrics reflected the distrust employees had for the way previous managers ran the center. The prior director espoused a "warm bodies in the seats" hiring ethic, and tolerated bad behavior. Standard operating procedures (SOPs) were just a suggestion. By failing to enforce rules, management allowed the center to become a place where people did not like to work.

This question addresses the values by which your center lives. Many centers don't take the time to specifically outline their behavioral values.

Instead, they operate on a default setting. Unfortunately, the default behavior is not usually the best. It's what's easy instead of what's necessary for success. It's easy to turn a blind eye to bad behavior and to just let things go.

Until it isn't.

The new director I quoted above was hired to solve specific issues. She was guided by her personal mission to make her center "a place where people want to work." With this guiding purpose, it was no longer possible to accept bad behavior. To do so would reflect an inability to hold *herself* accountable, and accountability was a value of great import.

When your center answers this question as fully as possible, these answers shape daily thoughts, behaviors, and interactions, and they have real power. To make their center a place where people want to work, the director and her team adhered to a system of values called CHAMPS.

CHAMPS:
- **C**hampion employees
- **H**onest communication
- **A**ccountability
- **M**ulti-cultural team
- **P**eople first
- **S**uperior services

By mirroring the values of the city government, the public safety dispatch center fell under, center leadership worked to contextualize these values in terms comm center staff could understand and use. This was rather easy, since city leadership had already done such a great job spelling out what the core values looked like as clear actions for city employees, in general, to take.

From the Sugar Land, TX, website:

> *Champion Employees*: Viewing employees as stakeholders; recognizing and encouraging valued behaviors; maintaining and improving a work culture that places an emphasis on employees' physical and mental well-being.

Honest and Open Communications: Open, honest and with respect; talk straight even when it is hard; really listen and hear what other people are saying.

Accountability: Owning our jobs; being responsible for our actions and behavior; fostering a culture of safety; cost-conscious; looking for innovated ways to save public funds; delivering results, not excuses; keeping commitments.

Multicultural: Being open and respectful of racial, generational, and cultural backgrounds of others; pursuing an understanding of other cultures in our community and organization.

People First: Building relationships with fellow employees; thinking in the best interest of others, even when it's difficult; taking time to know fellow employees; creating a family feel with our team and other employees.

Superior Service: Being responsive, honest, and accurate; planning well; following through on what we say we will do; being accommodating, considerate, courteous, and transparent.

If you don't articulate how your center's core values translate into acceptable (and unacceptable) behavior, this interpretation is left to the individual.

What Do We Do?

This question offers your comm center the opportunity to differentiate itself from the rest of the agency, department or organization it falls under. The answer to this question is the literal expression of *what* your center does—no adjectives or flowery language required. It is something clear and simple, such as "We answer calls for service" or "We provide quick and efficient assistance to our users."

It can be tempting to embellish or reach for abstract terms while answering this question, but it's important to keep this straightforward. Whereas the "why" is about the idealistic vision for the impact your center makes in the world, your "what" shouldn't be crafted so that it can also be used in marketing material. The exercise of clearly spelling out what your center *actually does* is designed to bring the leadership team into direct contact with the work at its purest definition.

How Will We Succeed?

Your center's success depends on the quality of the services your team provides, which flows from the people delivering that service. Strict adherence to policy and procedure does not automatically equate to quality service. It's all about the people.

People Driven Leaders help their teams define success and allow this team definition to guide strategy. To bring a team together and determine collectively how you will succeed requires that you answer the following questions:

1. Have you ever been part of a really great team?
2. What was different about this team?
3. How can we, as a team, create those kinds of feelings here?

Your team's answers to question 3 may include topics that address training, culture, communication, and others that set your center apart. What training does the team need to operate at a high level? How do you define excellence? This section is your leadership team's opportunity to define what truly makes your center special, and to come together around a shared set of priorities and a new way of thinking about them.

What Is Most Important, Right Now?

When Ivan Whitaker started at Polk County Communications in 2010, he knew he had to create ownership and buy-in or the consolidation effort would fail. Therefore, his immediate goal was to rebuild and grow trust throughout the organization. Every effort the leadership team made was devoted to this singular purpose.

In Patrick Lencioni's book *Silos, Politics and Turf Wars*, he calls the answer to this question a *thematic goal*: the single, temporary, and qualitative rallying cry shared by all leadership team members. A thematic goal should be something this team can accomplish in three to twelve months. Once the thematic goal has been set, the leadership team must carve out actionable steps to take during this timeframe that will ensure the goal is accomplished.

Who Must Do What?

This step involves identifying the people involved with the change: change agents, formal and informal leaders, and those who are bought in. Assign the tasks defined above to those involved in implementing change, and then begin. When a major cultural shift is the goal, it's important to spread the responsibility out to as many team members as possible.

In 2000, Carl Simpson was brought in to oversee the civilianization of leadership at Denver 9-1-1. As Director of Public Safety for Denver, he knew civilians needed to be the ones to do this job. "Right now," he said, "we're sending punished sergeants to serve their time in the radio room. The environment is ripe for negativity anyway, and then we're sending punished people there?"

The process was very involved. The director worked hand-in-hand with the police captain to replace 11 sergeants and to hire and select replacements for three lieutenants. The director was then to take over the captain's role. The city allotted 18 months for the transition.

There was immediate pushback from the assigned sergeants. They believed that handing over management duties to civilians would be akin to putting the inmates in charge of the asylum. The sergeants thought their command-and-control authoritarian leadership style was essential for protecting officers on the street. There was also pushback from tenured civilian employees in the center. They'd been hired under the outgoing management structure, so it was what they knew and what they liked, and they were comfortable with it.

In the early stages, Carl met with each of the 160 employees, along with every sergeant, lieutenant and the captain. It became obvious through these conversations that employees assumed that those currently designated as leads on the floor would become the supervisors and managers. Carl made it clear that this wasn't to be the case. He knew who had to do what for the initiative to succeed.

Instead of promoting all the current leads, one person was hired from the outside for every existing employee selected for a leadership role. The "that's the way we've always done it" culture was so strong that Carl knew without outside perspectives, the old ways would stick. And it was clear to most that the old ways were not working.

With civilian leadership, employee engagement skyrocketed. Instead of sergeants on punishment, the center had supervisors who were invested in their people. They were on the dispatch floor talking to them, helping them, and engaging team members on a personal level. Before the transition, call-takers were found to be on "not ready" 28% of the day. After the transition, "not ready" time had dropped to 6%. This was like adding 13 people to the staff. Realizing their negative attitude was no longer welcome, even the most difficult employees became converts.

SUMMARY: BRINGING THE VISION TO YOUR TEAM

The act of forming your vision and making it something your entire team can rally around requires asking yourself, your leadership team, and your staff these questions:

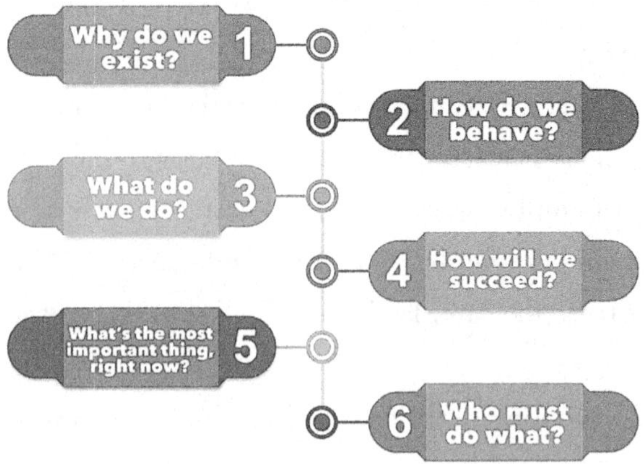

The above questions can seem difficult at first and may take some time to think through. It can help your team to kick off the process of envisioning possibilities if you complete this exercise:

Team Vision Exercise

1. Have you ever been a part of a really great team?

You can define "a really great team" any way you like—but it should be a team where you felt personally committed, where you signed up fully, and where the team achieved extraordinary results. Think back to that experience.

2. What was different about this team?

Talk about what felt truly special about being on that "really great" team. Have a scribe write all significant comments down on a flipchart.

3. How can we, as a team, create those kinds of feelings here?

What could we do [achieve, accomplish, create together] that would rekindle the same feelings we remember from those "really great teams"?

4. What would we commit ourselves to?

What initiatives and individual commitments matter most for the way forward? Set priorities and think about them in a new way.

CHAPTER 8

TRUST IS MORE THAN A FEELING

Creating a unifying mission and a compelling vision can be transformative as an exercise unto itself. Unfortunately, some centers stop there. They post their freshly crafted mission statement on the wall and declare, "This is the standard!" But after a few weeks, the motivation wears off, and things return to the way they were before. For this work to really pay, what happens next is most important. You have to make your vision real.

Making your mission and vision more than just a nifty new wall hanging takes action. You must begin building (or rebuilding) trust. You must communicate frequently and practice radical transparency. Integrity must flow through from the top down, all the while taking care to proactively manage the transition. Embracing a renewed level of accountability and practicing it every day will inspire others to hold themselves and each other accountable.

TURNING VISION INTO RESULTS

After surveys indicated that 98% of staff at the comm center had no confidence in their center's management, control of North Little Rock Emergency Management and 9-1-1 was temporarily given to the Police Department. In mid-2015, retired Police Captain Leonard Montgomery was asked to run this new department, which included Emergency Management and 9-1-1 Communications. A 38-year veteran of PD, he had a reputation for improving and changing things, and the Communications staff was excited to have him come aboard. In early 2016, Leonard took over as department head.

He reported directly to the mayor as a department head, so PD no longer had any oversight.

Leonard was appointed because of his reputation as a People Driven Leader. "I try to look out for my people," he said, "because I can't do this myself. Our people are our greatest asset." North Little Rock was in tough shape from a people perspective. With nearly zero confidence in management before Leonard came aboard, staffing had dropped to 15 employees from 25. Already familiar with the challenges this group faced, Leonard took decisive action quickly.

The department immediately allocated $40,000 on things that showed they were making progress. They bought new computer monitors. They got the vehicle location maps working. Leonard also set appointments to meet with everyone, to hear their concerns, and to clearly communicate the expectations moving forward. He outlined what needed to change and communicated what needed to happen in order for this change to take place. In these one-on-ones, he reassured people that he was not looking to fire anyone. "You all have an equal opportunity to succeed," he told them. "It's my job to create an environment where success is possible."

Leonard took several steps to create this environment. He did a salary survey. He found that while most employees had essentially *volunteered* for supervisor at some point, they hadn't been supported in their role. One area reflecting this lack of support was pay. Previously, supervisors were paid $0.35 more—that's 35 CENTS more per hour—to step into the role. Based on the results of the salary survey, supervisor pay was raised to several more dollars per hour.

Leonard also found that the center had never used employee recognition programs. When employees got awards for tenure or work well done, there was no presentation or personal acknowledgment. Instead, envelopes were slid in their mailboxes. Now, people are recognized every step of the way. Presentations are done personally, visibly and regularly.

The results of Leonard's approach speak volumes. He stepped fully into the role in January of 2016. By September of 2017, the center was fully staffed. That's 20 months to cure a problem that persisted for years before.

It was by no means easy. In the first year, 18 people left the center—a 72% annual turnover rate! When Leonard sat down with each employee and communicated his expectations, he told his team certain behaviors would no longer be tolerated. Among them was harassment and bullying. When people heard that Leonard was coming out of retirement to head the department, four previous team members—who had left because of the center's former management—came back to work for the center. They ended up being some of the biggest bullies, and they were still on probation when they began demonstrating this behavior. They were asked to leave the department before the end of their probationary period. Other tenured employees also resigned while under investigation for contributing to the old problems. Once Leonard set the standard, communicated the expectations, and began holding people accountable, things changed dramatically.

I asked Bud Gray, Deputy Commander at North Little Rock, what Leonard did to inspire the changes the center has seen in the last couple years. The first thing he expressed was the initial concern the team felt around having the captain as their newly appointed leader. "We thought PD was going to take over, and that would be the end of it," Bud said. Instead, the positive changes were felt almost immediately. "The biggest differences between how things were and how they are now is employee recognition and management style. The Captain treats us with respect and consistent fairness. He knows that everyone wants to be heard, loved, and respected, and this flows through his leadership approach."

In addition to Leonard and his Deputy, I had the chance to speak with a team member who left a neighboring comm center to work at North Little Rock. It's not uncommon for dispatchers to join the ranks of another center, but the circumstances surrounding this departure and hire are surprising. One team member in particular took a $10,000 pay cut to join the North Little Rock team. "Why would you do that!?" I asked her. "Management is different here," she said. As a result, "there's rapport between us team members, and we all help each other out. My coworkers and I know that we sink each other or lift each other up. We choose to lift each other."

The people driven approach that management models sets the tone for everyone else to follow. I love the story of North Little Rock because it teaches so many lessons. It shows the power of setting a standard, communicating these expectations, and holding people accountable. As one of my supervisors at LAPD would always say, "We talk about it, so let's be about it." North Little Rock's story also shows how these things begin to pay dividends more valuable than money. Yes, we have to pay a nominal wage that's comparable to what other centers in the area pay, but pay matters less than we tend to admit.

Another few lessons are contained in Leonard's final statements to me. "I'm not a great leader by any means; I still work at it," he said, emphasizing the humility of this type of leader. "I try to look out for my people, because I can't do this myself—personnel are the greatest asset," he continued. "I approach things from the standpoint that they can be fixed. If you say [something] can't be fixed, you set yourself up to fail."

PUTTING FIRST THINGS FIRST

Once you have a clear vision and thematic goal that exposes a path of action, it's time to start down that path. The execution can be the most difficult. It requires decisiveness, persistence and at times, blind faith. Success was anything but certain for any of the leaders featured here. They had faith their actions would eventually produce results, but in some cases, it was years before that faith was rewarded with the hoped-for culture shift. A clear vision can provide the impulse to act, even if the steps aren't that clear. The people who are most effective during this stage are also able to adapt while in constant flux. People Driven Leaders inspire high performance culture by building trust, by communicating effectively, and by managing the transition along the way.

A CERTAIN KIND OF TRUST

As children, we implicitly trust everyone. Not knowing danger, our natural disposition is to trust that people will meet our expectations. We trust they won't let us down. Of course, the more life experience we gain, the more we discover this isn't true. When we're wronged as children, we don't see it as being "wronged." Instead, these experiences shape both how we view ourselves and the world at large. Subtly, we come to believe that people are a certain way.

We don't question whether these beliefs are right or wrong. They are simply the way we see things. As an adult at work, we know there are topics we'd rather avoid because they make us feel uncomfortable. This uncomfortableness ripples out from our emotional triggers or hot buttons. If something rubs up against these deeply held beliefs, we'll react in some way. An emotion arises in the body; frustration or rage causes us to lash out. The effect may result in something less perceptible.

For example, someone says something that seems harmless at first, but the more we brood on it, the more worked up we get. A spouse or loved one never expresses appreciation and regularly belittles us. The new job is ok at first, but as we learn more about the way people talk to each other, the negativity causes us to adopt a cynical attitude as well. We come to certain realizations gradually as we understand a situation more deeply. Often, all this is going on without us knowing. We're sizing things up, judging, feeling certain ways about certain things, and actions flow from these judgements. This process is subtle, gradual and powerful. It is the effect of our emotional constitution on daily work life.

The seat of emotion is the limbic brain. Also called the reptilian brain, this part of the brain was the first to evolve. At the very center of the gray mass contained in your skull is where the fight-or-flight response lives. It governs survival. When the limbic brain is activated, it becomes much more difficult to think creatively about situations. If you're in fear for your life (or so thinks the brain), only survival matters. A perception of danger awakens this ancient machinery and prevents anything else from getting through.

Think about the last time something really stressed you out. Where did you feel it in the body? What happened to your ability to think critically or logically? During the most stressful times—when danger feels imminent—we become locked in fight, flight or freeze mode, unable to respond normally.

In life at the comm center, the limbic brain affects us in more subtle ways. If we don't trust the people we work for and with, we may feel continuously stressed. Over time, we burn out and check out. This can happen when we feel left in the dark because decisions are made without our input; it can happen when we don't have an avenue for giving and receiving feedback, or when the work environment is hostile.

Essentially, a lack of trust means we feel unsafe, both in the personal and organizational environments. At its core, organizational trust is feeling like the center you work for has your best interests in mind. People Driven Leaders are best at creating that "Circle of Safety." These exemplary leaders foster inclusion and buy-in, bringing everyone—up, down and across the organization—on board with the day-to-day.

In his book *Overcoming the 5 Dysfunctions of a Team,* Patrick Lencioni calls "absence of trust" the first dysfunction of team. He points out that only by creating trust can we overcome it. Lencioni further defines a certain type of trust. This isn't the type of trust you share with an old friend or family member, where you might be able to predict how they're feeling based on how they look or talk that day. The type of trust essential for high-performing teams is called *vulnerability-based trust*.

There are several components to building this type of trust. The most important are communication and integrity. These boil down to sharing what you're going to do, what the expectations moving forward are, and then taking action. In an industry where much of what happens is outside the span of control for those on the front line, constant communication is essential for providing a feeling of safety during times of change.

A lack of frequent communication allows gossip and rumors to fill the void. To quell the feelings of apprehension and distrust, a team splits into factions of dysfunction. These factions offer a feeling of safety that isn't there otherwise. Venting and complaining along with people who share your viewpoint can be comforting. Misery loves company, after all.

Regular communication is the antidote for gossip and the negativity it spews. The best centers communicate at least on a weekly basis. One director makes it a point to spend time on the dispatch floor daily, talking with her people. This exemplary leader sees these informal meetings as her opportunity to get to know her team on a personal level. Another center uses a weekly "all-leadership" meeting to bring lead dispatchers, supervisors, and the director together to discuss how the center is doing in relation to its metrics for success. This keeps the team's goals in sight and offers a chance to course-correct if needed.

Committing to frequent communication also insures there's an opportunity to catch your people doing good work. So often, the only time we hear anything is when it's negative. It's often said that the public safety industry is reactive. This reactive stance is connected to only having enough time to put out fires (both literal and figurative). Adopting a proactive approach to communication can help fight this negative focus.

Frequent communication also increases transparency. In his classic book *Verbal Judo,* Dr. George Thompson says that one of the five universal truths about people is that "everyone wants to know why they're being asked to do something." Providing employees context for the decisions being made—especially when these decisions impact daily work life—is essential for creating a culture of trust and loyalty. When there's complete transparency, even if the team doesn't like what's said, at least they know what's going on.

Self-Assessment:

1. Where is your center lacking in the area of communication?
2. How can you be more transparent on a daily/weekly basis?
3. What else might you be able to do to inspire a greater degree of vulnerability-based trust in your teams?

While doing comm center culture assessments, my team uses an anonymous survey to ask these difficult questions. When phrased in a specific way and asked while granting anonymity, center staff is likely to share exactly what they think of the way leadership communicates, along with potential improvement points. There are several inexpensive online resources for administering such surveys.

CHAPTER 9

A BETTER WAY TO COMMUNICATE

If frequent communication is the basis for building trust, we should probably spend a little time discussing the *kind* of communication we're talking about, because certainly, not all communication has the power to build trust and cultivate loyalty. On the contrary, if we don't watch our words and how we say them, we may have the opposite effect, ruining relationships and adding to a negative culture.

For people who are professionally in "communications," I marvel at how poorly emergency communications personnel communicate with each other at work (and at home). Why is it this way? There are few factors that contribute to our (that is, humans') inability to communicate.

First, we've been speaking since a very young age. We take it for granted! This communication thing is more complicated than we'd like to admit, and instead of saying, "Hmm, maybe *I'm* the one who's not very good at expressing myself," we take the easy way out and blame the person across the table. "I'd be a much better communicator if I wasn't surrounded by idiots!" we exclaim in frustration.

In addition to taking its complexity for granted, most of our personal communication history began when we started modeling the communication strategies of our parents or guardians. Especially in heated exchanges where emotions run high, if the methods our moms and dads used weren't exactly productive, it's possible we're using them in similar unproductive fashion.

I don't know about you, but my parents were severely deficient when it came to resolving conflict. I learned by watching them that it's best to just walk away when things get heated. Instead of adeptly navigating conflict and using these challenges as growth opportunities, I had a habit of just letting things fester, being passive-aggressive, and then watching interpersonal situations blow up in my face down the road.

Another factor preventing positive interaction is that many people don't place enough importance on good communication. If we knew that improving the quality of our communication could improve our home life, work life, and make us more money, we'd probably be doing a lot more each day to get better at it. Several studies show that better communicators not only create a better workplace, but they get more of what they want as well. Further, leaders who are the most effective communicators build relationships based on vulnerability and trust, even in the midst of conflict.

Which of the above factors may be influencing your communication? It's not easy to acknowledge areas for improvement, but it's impossible to improve without doing so.

Contemplating and then understanding our role in negative interactions is the beginning of improving emotional intelligence. Employees with a high degree of emotional intelligence are automatically going to be better communicators. Some of the best 9-1-1 centers value emotional intelligence so highly that it is an essential factor in their hiring and training processes. One center I know of requires emotional intelligence training for all new supervisors. They take an assessment and then create a personal plan for developing more emotional intelligence. And truly, life is so much easier when you're able to work skillfully with emotional situations, both at work and at home, which underscores the power of prioritizing personal improvement in this area for anyone.

THE EMOTIONALLY INTELLIGENT COMMUNICATOR

As mentioned in the first section, there are four skills of emotional intelligence, and each imparts a greater ability to communicate.

1. Self-Awareness
2. Self-Management
3. Social Awareness
4. Relationship Management/Social Skills

Improving one's self-awareness is the start of something big, as it enhances our ability to make a positive difference. By improving my self-awareness, I can see my impact on the people I come in contact with, and I can make adjustments if that effect is less than stellar. Some simple ways to improve self-awareness include asking others for feedback, taking some time to sit and breathe for five minutes each day, and writing in a journal.

Self-awareness improves one's communication ability because you're less likely to say things that would lead to a communication breakdown when you've understood your role in such a breakdown in the past. If you notice you have a tendency to be short with people when you're feeling tired or anxious, you might put off engaging a difficult conversation until you're feeling better able to work with such a situation. This is how self-awareness leads to self-management.

Simple ways to improve self-management include hitting the "pause" in whatever way you're able: go to the bathroom, take a breath, put the caller on hold. Saying no to things you'd rather not be doing is another way to create some space. Any time you think before you speak, you're demonstrating self-management.

Simple ways to improve social awareness include talking with the people you work with and noticing what's going on with them. While engaged in a conversation, truly listening can help you understand others more fully. The next time you enter the comm center, notice the tone of the room. Are people happy? Is there another emotion apparent? Improving this aspect of your awareness can make it easier to have difficult conversations and to bolster the case for doing so more frequently. Practice helps with anything.

To improve relationship management is to acknowledge another person's feelings. It can be something as simple as saying, "I'm sorry you're feeling this way. Is there anything I can do?" Showing genuine interest in the people you work with can build connection and make life much easier. Explaining your decisions, especially when occupying a leadership role, is another relationship management strategy you can use.

Conflict is inevitable at the comm center. Without emotional intelligence, it's nearly impossible to get anything good out of it. We always lose something when we're unable to navigate conflict productively. We may miss a solution to a perennial problem. An employee who doesn't feel heard may decide to leave the organization. If nothing else, we may keep our old worn-out way of thinking intact. Conflict *can* offer an opportunity, but only when we approach it in an emotionally intelligent way. It's a chance to find common ground and to build rapport. Without conflict, we don't learn anything about another's perspective.

Think about it: when everything is going "well" at work—employees are having fun, everyone's doing their job, the days are easy—we don't actually know what others are thinking. During the good times, we can pretty much assume that everyone is thinking something similar. When there's a conflict, we are given a window into a different viewpoint.

To get the most out of these exchanges—or any communication exchange, for that matter—it helps to follow a few guidelines.

1. **Check your listening.** How do you tend to show up for a communication exchange? Are you thinking of your reply, waiting for the other person to shut up so you can talk— or are you actively engaged in what he or she is saying? What story does your body language and other non-verbals tell? Are your arms crossed, reflecting your closedness to the

situation? Are you leaning in a bit, demonstrating your clear interest? Do you look down when eye contact would be more effective? How distracted are you? Is your phone dominating your attention? Are you listening through judgement and filters?

Going into a conversation ready to listen—to really *listen*—can help the exchange get off to a good start. This is sometimes the most difficult part because of the job we do, because we're not necessarily paid to listen. We're paid to get information quickly. Building connection by exchanging thoughts and ideas is a different skill-set, one that many in 9-1-1 aren't very good at and have to consciously work on.

2. **Prepare ahead of time.** Especially before going into an exchange that covers a sensitive matter, this is not the time to "wing it." Much of our inability to navigate conflict comes from the fact that we don't do it often. Sit down beforehand and write some questions that offer deeper introspection than defensive responses. Consider the best possible outcome for this exchange, and plan according to this. Do you need more information before proceeding?

3. **Put yourself in the other person's shoes.** How would you respond to the same feedback? What would make this the most productive exchange for both parties? We tend to lose touch of how it felt to experience similar challenges, unable to bridge the "empathy gap," because we underestimate the difficulty of the challenge to the person who isn't us.

4. **Ask for feedback.** After the exchange, ask your counterpart if they have any further questions for you and whether they thought the feedback was valuable or productive. If you have the courage to ask for feedback after

offering criticism or feedback of your own, be sure you are open to receiving and acting upon it.

Communicating effectively and doing it often stimulates a culture of accountability while serving as the glue that holds a high-performing team together. With compassion and curiosity, comm center leaders can transform the most challenging discussions into opportunities for growth—on both sides of the table.

Self-Assessment

1. We often receive signs as to whether we are communicating effectively. Do you think people generally perceive you as an effective communicator, or are there areas where you can improve?
2. In which ways might you be able to improve your communication?

CHAPTER 10

INTEGRITY IN ACTION

Along with increasing transparency through frequent communication, the other element of building organizational trust is establishing integrity. While it's cited by many people and organizations as a core value, it's one thing to *say* that integrity matters, and it's quite another to live it daily.

Many people tend to think of integrity only in the context of legal and illegal activity. Clearly, running an NCIC wanted-persons check on a prospective love interest outside the course of duty is unethical, illegal and shows a lack of integrity. Using your agency's affiliation for personal gain is another obvious no-no. But if these and similarly obvious transgressions are the only situations that meet our qualification for unethical conduct and questionable integrity, we are likely missing a large swath of everyday goings-on affecting how employees feel about the organization.

I recently facilitated a team-building training day for a PSAP's leadership team. This is an excellent PSAP, staffed by dedicated professionals who truly care about their work and the community they serve. Everyone on the leadership team shares this dedication and has done a lot of work together to improve morale and the center's culture. One example of this is their "Core Values, Mission Statement, and Code of Conduct" document. They are proud of this document and what it stands for, and they require every employee to sign it and to know its contents.

About halfway through the team-building day, I distributed a copy of this document to each member of the leadership team and had them read it carefully, considering every word. After a few minutes, I asked, "How do you think we're doing as a team upholding these words?"

After a long silence, one of the supervisors said, "Sadly, not very well." The rest of the team echoed this sentiment and began detailing the ways they lacked integrity in the mismatch of their core values and code of conduct. They mentioned how the code of conduct expressly discussed how they want to be treated by each other, and how they are missing the mark most days.

This team has a document that professes what they stand for. But no one is adhering to it. What does this do to the organization? What message does it send to new and tenured employees, alike?

For example, a trainee is required to sign for and memorize the core values and code of conduct. By signing, the trainee agrees to uphold the integrity of the organization's code, along with all the other employees. This is no small ask. The organization's leaders are essentially requiring the employee to agree to a set of principles and values determining right and wrong, with the knowledge that if they do not, something will happen. In the military, there are stiff penalties for refusing to obey codes of conduct, including dismissal and criminal prosecution.

After signing this document and understanding its importance, the trainee begins working in the center and starts to notice something. One of the bullet points in the code of conduct specifically mentions maintaining a professional image. The definition of the image includes no gossip, bullying or character assassination—both towards the public and fellow coworkers. The trainee notices that some of the more tenured employees at the center gossip daily, complain about other coworkers and callers, and otherwise create a toxic work atmosphere. No one says anything, and it seems like this is just normal behavior.

At this point, the trainee can make one of several choices. She can say something to one of her supervisors about the clear disregard for the code she's witnessed. She can mention something to the tenured employee. She can join in the behavior, disregarding the code herself, even though it's still fresh in her mind. She can just keep working, hoping that things get better. Or, she can quit her new job in the hopes she finds something better.

Organizational integrity is determined by how closely we follow the decisions made around policy and procedure, values and mission. When we don't do what we say we're going to do, trust erodes. Over years, this lack of trust becomes an aspect of the organization's culture. Eventually, people do just the bare minimum and abuse sick time; cynicism runs rampant, and morale sucks. Without understanding the deeper effects of not doing what we say we're going to do, we may be tempted to say, "This is just the way things are," and resign ourselves to hating our workplace until we can find something else better. This is the current state of affairs many comm centers are facing.

Ideally, a center's code of conduct, informed by its core values, is the stake in the ground, the line in the sand, and the point from which all other pieces of organizational life flow. A code of conduct can be an important part in establishing an inclusive culture, but it is not a comprehensive solution on its own. Studies of codes of conduct in the private sector show that their **effective implementation** must be part of a learning process that requires training, consistent enforcement, and continuous measurement/improvement. Simply requiring members to read and sign for the code is not enough to ensure they understand it and will remember what it really means for the organization.

Integrity is demonstrated by, and the result of, a continuous flow. The flow at your agency might look like this:

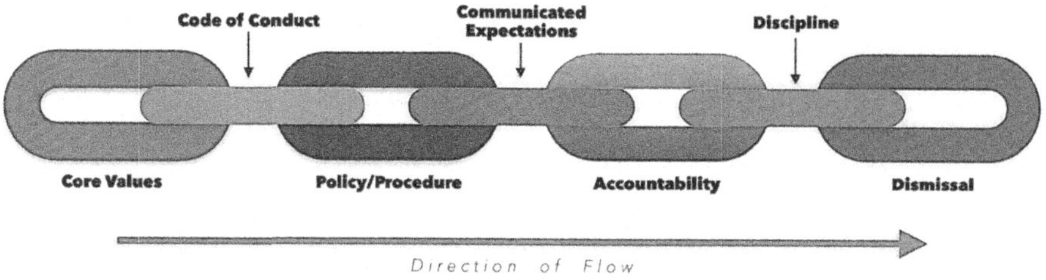

Like links in a chain, if one of these pieces is weak or missing, the entire chain is broken. It no longer works. It is not merely enough to do the bare minimum. Doing the bare minimum in public safety—not breaking the law or not violating a clear policy (i.e., sending units on a ringing alarm)—is easy. It's also easy to hold people accountable to this bare minimum, because things are so black and white. You either broke the law or didn't. You either followed the policy or didn't (even though some agencies falter on even these easy-to-make calls for accountability).

Following a code of conduct and observing the organization's core values, as they apply to the people working side-by-side inside the comm center, is a bit more nuanced. It's colored with shades of gray and personal perceptions, which is why it isn't easy.

From a personal standpoint, the importance of trust can't be overstated. Without trust, a relationship is doomed. It seems that we think about trust differently in an organizational setting, yet the research on organizational trust shows that morale is higher when there is trust. Organizations high in trust perform at a higher level. In short, trust helps stuff get done.

Self-Assessment

1. In which area is your center most out of integrity, or the most in need of change?
2. What are your team's perception of this state, and the changes required?
3. What can you do today to begin to correct this break in the chain?

CHAPTER 11

THE ART OF MANAGING TRANSITIONS

There's another dimension of trust that's important to consider. Do you trust your people enough to give them something to own? Do you delegate freely and empower often? Without trust, change is impossible. This type of empowerment helps teams drive change instead of being taken out by it.

Let's say you have a room of type A perfectionist dispatchers who are good at what they do. They take pride in the job they perform and thrive in the adrenaline-soaked confines of a center working a major incident. It takes months or years to get good at the job, and then a change is introduced: a new policy, adding another screen, or the worst-possible case: a consolidation.

By its very definition, change produces anxiety. Think about what happens when change is introduced. The fear of failure arises. No matter who you are, stepping outside of the familiar creates an uncomfortable feeling. To work through these feelings—to help the organization even thrive while amidst them—takes a certain leadership approach, one that helps cultivate trust in the possibility of rising to the occasion.

In his book *Managing Transitions: Making the Most of Change*, author William Bridges says that making the most out of change is the simple process of helping people through three phases:

1. **Letting go of the old ways** and the old identity people had. This first phase of transition is an ending; it is when you need to help people to deal with their losses.

2. **Going through an in-between time** when the old is gone but the new isn't fully operational. Bridges calls this time the "neutral zone": it's when the critical psychological realignments and repatterning take place.
3. Coming out of the transition and **making a new beginning**. This is when people develop the new identity, experience the new energy, and discover the new sense of purpose that make the change begin to work.

Any change requires effectively managing this transition, from old to new. Because of this, we can say that transition starts with an ending and finishes with a beginning. Changes of any sort succeed or fail based on whether the people affected do things differently. Do the employees let go of the old way of doing things, undergo that difficult time between the old way and the new, and come out doing things the new way? If leaders don't help people through these three phases, even the most wonderful plans fall flat. In these scenarios, leaders forget the ending and neutral zones; they try to start with the final stage of transition, and they are unable to see what went wrong!

Ivan Whitaker knew at Polk County that if he were to slam two comm centers together without preparing his people properly, the consolidation effort would be a dismal failure. So, he instead sat down with every single employee, one-on-one, and gave them each an opportunity to share their concerns. He then explained the upcoming process. To quell the anxiety around the upcoming widespread changes, he gave them as much information as he had. He shared timelines and other specifics, with as much advanced notice as possible, so they had time to process and adjust. He was helping them cope with the first phase.

During the second phase, Whitaker convened committees to create and implement solutions to the problems front line employees were experiencing. They worked through the "neutral zone" as a team, fashioning a new way forward. This part of the transition took about two years. During this two-year period, nearly everyone was involved in enacting the changes. In time, the talk about what the comm center *was* disappeared. "We went from talking about how bad things [had been] to talking about positive changes, and how we could continue to change things for the better," Ivan said.

The transition from ruminating about what was "lost" to applauding the positive changes currently taking place marked the step into phase three, which is characterized by a new identity and energy surrounding the change.

MISMANAGED TRANSITION

In a different area of the country, a bungled consolidation effort provided further evidence to the front line that "they don't care about us, and it's just about the almighty dollar." In this situation, center management held no future-oriented discussions with employees before consolidation. They made no efforts to solve current problems proactively in an effort to ensure that they didn't also become tomorrow's problems. Managers at the two centers targeted for consolidation notified their people of the pending consolidation. They focused primarily on the technology side of the effort, making sure the telephones and computers worked properly, ensuring there were seats and consoles for the bodies in the room. Then, one day, the two teams were brought under one roof.

It wasn't surprising to learn that the teams from both centers felt neglected by management *pre-consolidation*, and that these feelings of neglect continued into the current organizational situation. It's also probably not surprising to share that today, years after the consolidation, employees are still talking about how poorly the effort went, and how much of their original identity was lost during the process. Without taking into consideration what is being lost (and rightly mourned) during sweeping changes, the change effort will likely fail.

THE MOST IMPORTANT STEPS

If there's one thing that's constant in this industry, it's that it's changing. Technology has always been changing rapidly, but 9-1-1 is finally catching up. As a result, 9-1-1 will be forced to keep up with this rapid-fire pace as a new normal. To get the hoped-for benefit of any change, the initial steps are the most important.

First, **figure out exactly how individuals' behavior and attitudes will have to change to make teams work**. It isn't enough to direct your people to "work as a team." If they knew how to do it, it would already be happening. They need to know how teamwork differs behaviorally and attitudinally from the way they are working now. Be specific about what they must stop doing and what they must start doing. Until you spell out these changes, people won't be able to understand what you tell them.

Next, **analyze who stands to lose something under the new way of doing things**. Remember, transition starts with an ending. You can't grasp the new thing until you've let go of the old thing. It's the process of letting go that people resist, not the change itself. Their resistance can take the form of foot-dragging or sabotage, and you have to understand the pattern of loss to be ready to deal with the resistance and to keep it from getting out of hand.

Then, **"sell" the problem that is the reason for change.** Most managers and leaders put 10% of their energy into selling the problem and 90% into selling the solution to the problem. People don't care about the solutions to problems they don't see, acknowledge, and understand. They might even come up with a better solution, and then you won't have to sell it, because it'll be theirs.

Talk to your people. Many managers assume they know why certain problem exist, when they actually don't have the foggiest idea. Ask them about the problems they're currently experiencing and the cause of them. Ask the right questions; open-ended ones, like, "What's your perspective on things?" or "I'd love to get your take on our situation," work well to start a conversation and show a willingness to listen. If you ask, "Why aren't you doing this?" you've set up an adversarial dynamic and will probably get a defensive answer.

Talk about what transition does to people. Give supervisors and others involved the initiative training on how to make it successful. Everyone can benefit from understanding transition. Supervisors will deal with employees better if they understand what the employees are going through. If they understand what transition feels like, team members will feel more confident that they haven't taken a wrong turn.

Start holding regular team meetings. Even before you start moving furniture, you can start building the new identity by having teams meet regularly. Especially with a big change, frequent pow-wows can override the old habits and build the new relationships that teamwork requires. If it's important, give it a visible place on the calendar and then prioritize the time to bring people together.

In their enthusiasm for a future that is going to be better than the past, many managers ridicule or talk disparagingly of the old way of doing things. But doing so only encourages resistance against the transition. People identify with the way things used to be and thus feel that their self-worth is at stake whenever the past is attacked. French writer Anatole France put it succinctly when he wrote, "All changes, even the most longed for, have their melancholy; for what we leave behind is part of ourselves; we must die one life before we can enter into another."

Leaders who honor the passing of the old ways, even if the ways weren't that efficient to begin with, help model the respect and openness required by all team members for a transition to be successful.

In their classic book *The Leadership Challenge*, authors James Kouzes and Barry Posner write that exemplary leaders "enable others to act" by fostering collaboration and strengthening others. It's an important quality at any time, but critical during times of change. Change causes people to look out only for themselves. With feelings of uncertainty running rampant, survival is all that matters. When they're in survival mode, employees are less likely to reach out to team members they don't know that well to invent solutions. To fight this tendency, the best leaders bring people together, get them necessary training, and keep the focus on the vision of possibility.

GIVE THEM SOMETHING TO OWN

I've seen centers as small as 25 full-time employees have lead dispatchers, tactical dispatchers, five supervisors, an ops manager, QA manager and a director. How can they justify so many levels of the organization with so few people? They know the power of creating buy-in. When someone is specifically accountable for something—especially when that someone is a type A perfectionist—they are going to dedicate themselves with much more passion for the role.

You can't—nor should you try to—navigate change alone. Ivan Whitaker's success at Polk County Sheriffs was due in large part to the fact that he delegated the responsibility for the transition to many members of the team. They felt part of something. They helped create the future instead of feeling like unwitting victims of yet another change.

When team members believe they are a part of creating something that is theirs, a marked shift happens—away from "problem-solving" towards "opportunity-seeking." Ivan Whitaker noticed something similar as the transition took on a life of its own.

QUANTIFY THE INTANGIBLES

People often assume that we can't measure the softer side of organizational life. Ideas like culture, morale, and core values tend to fall by the wayside as managers focus on "hard" statistics like call service levels, shift coverage and new technology. One manager I spoke with said that staffing was her major challenge, and there was nothing else they could focus on until the center was fully staffed. She was hesitant to offer training for her existing staff because it was unclear to her how spending money on training would impact her ability to recruit, hire, train and keep new employees.

Many centers are in a similar limbo. Stuck in a perpetual loop of minimum staffing and forced OT, there's no headspace for proactive measures like training and recognition. The problem with thinking that you must wait until the center is fully staffed to take proactive measures is that it is likely the *current lack* of proactive measures preventing the center from being fully staffed. Most people won't stay at a job where they don't feel valued, heard, respected.

It's the intangibles that make an organization worth working for. From the outset, people don't *really* care about whether the center is "making its numbers." Knowing that call-service levels are meeting the minimum standard is not an exciting motivator for anyone, even the supervisors who are tasked with making sure the numbers are being met. Has anyone gone home and celebrated with friends the fact that the center answered 91% of emergency calls within 10 seconds today? Probably not.

On the other hand, employees *have* gone home feeling uplifted by the teamwork they experienced during their workday. They've been inspired by the difference they see themselves and their teammates making for the people and the communities they serve. They've felt the pride of knowing they helped officers catch the bad guy or coached a caller through life-saving CPR instructions.

The uplifting, motivating forces in any job—like inspiration, purpose, pride, making a difference—are intangible. The numbers may be interesting, to a few...but, in general, the hard data aren't what makes a center a great place to work. The numbers are a *reflection* of a great (or less-than-great) place to work. The intangibles are what makes it great. And despite their intangibility, these important factors *can* be measured. In more than one of my interviews with exemplary comm center leaders, they've said, "You MUST quantify the intangibles."

In fact, they're so important that if you don't quantify them, you won't know why people leave. Departing employees won't say in an exit interview, "I'm leaving because this organization seems out of alignment with its professed values." "I'm looking for more integrity from the place I work." "People sure treat each other like shit around here."

They'll instead say, "This just isn't what I expected." "I want more time with my family." Or they won't say anything at all.

The intangibles are all about the 'F' word. *Not that F word!* They're about *feelings*.

When we seek to quantify the intangibles, we're really asking people how they *feel* about the place they work. Motivation is a feeling. Pride, satisfaction, purpose—all feelings. One manager said, "I can't make my employees happy. However, it's my job to provide an environment where happiness is possible." This manager knows the importance of how his employees feel about coming into work each day. He's also acutely aware of how his actions (or lack thereof) impact this feeling. How does he know this? He's in constant communication with his people.

ASK FOR FEEDBACK — TALK TO YOUR PEOPLE!

The easiest way to understand how people feel about working at the center is to ask them. All of the exemplary leaders I interviewed for this book told me some variation of this. One said, "My first focus is my people. My job is to make their jobs easier. I'm constantly listening to them." Another said, "I work for my people, not the other way around. I learn about their families, try to understand what makes them tick, and learn how I can help them." Yet another said, "The way I inspire trust is communication! I communicate, communicate, communicate. But it has to be in the right way."

People Driven Leaders take some time, every day, to walk the floor and learn what's going on. They genuinely care about and are concerned for their people, and this concern flows into these interactions.

What if you'd like to start having these conversations, but you don't know where to start? I find that many in leadership roles are prevented from making a genuine connection with their employees because they fear judgement, or saying the wrong thing, or not being accepted. It can be difficult to ask someone for their opinion when you worry about what they might say. No one likes criticism, so rather than open ourselves up to it, we opt to stay in the office instead. While the fear of judgement becomes the underlying feeling, we add a layer of excuses on top to ignore or conceal what's really going on.

"Yeah, sure, it would be nice to know what people on the floor are thinking," we say, "but I've got too much work to do. I can't spend hours on the dispatch floor just *talking* with people."

The excuse in this statement is, "I've got too much work." The reality is that we fear feedback, especially when it feels like a personal attack. I asked LaDonna Coriell, former Marshall County E911 Director, what she suggests when people say, "I'd like to make a positive change, but I don't have the time/support from management/etc." LaDonna put it succinctly: "Every manager is going to spend time in areas where they think it's important. I've found I can spend five minutes getting to know my people, or I can spend hours working on complaints and other punitive action, like I used to. Prioritizing your people takes away the other time-consuming tasks I'd rather not have to spend my time on."

Contained in this statement is the power of a proactive approach. You can spend 5-10 minutes each day proactively talking with your people, or you can wait until they do something questionable and reactively take punitive action. Prioritizing proactivity requires a fundamental shift in thinking. The common approach is, "If it ain't broke, don't fix it," which leads to a "hands-off" approach. This approach is actually helpful when you've delegated a specific task of which someone has direct ownership. But taking the temperature of the room, so to speak, is never a hands-off matter. In fact, if no one is taking the time to solicit feedback about the perceived reality, you shouldn't be surprised when you don't hear anything.

After years of not asking, you may be met with another challenge. You ask, but no one says anything. All you get is canned, one-syllable responses. "Good." "Fine." "Ok." In this case, it may take some time to prime the pump. This phase is about trust-building. One new director took his initial days on the job to sit down with every one of his employees one-on-one and to ask them point-blank what the problems at the center were and what they thought the solutions were. At first, they wouldn't open up. For years, the former director had said, "We'd love to do something, but our hands are tied." Employees expected more of the same. So, the director started by sharing some of *his* vision of the improvements he was going to make. He assured his new team that he was there to make things better. In time, they opened up. They got involved with the process. They were given hope again (another intangible *feeling*).

On the same token, people may be fearful that if they say what they really think, the information could be used against them at a later time. In this case, providing reassurance that that isn't the case and taking measures to create a feeling of safety will go the furthest. We've all worked for a fear-based micromanager who is more interested in their personal gain (or what they have to lose) than team dynamics. Burned from these past experiences, it can take a little work to establish a connection. The best leaders know that it's all about relationships, and every one of these exchanges has the power to build them up or tear them down.

The important thing, especially when you don't get the real story, is to keep trying. I hear this often in my leadership classes. "I've tried everything, but it still doesn't work! Our culture is still toxic and morale sucks," one supervisor said. This can definitely be frustrating, especially when your heart is in the right place. Try a different approach, a new line of questioning. Just don't give up. Trust takes a long time to build, but once it's there, it's amazing what can happen.

TURN TO THE METRICS

While establishing meaningful relationships that allow communication (and information) to freely flow up, down and across the organization, we also have to look at the metrics that reflect how people feel about where they work.

When taken together with the face-to-face conversations, a clear picture will emerge.

The best centers regularly track the following metrics and talk about them in team meetings. They set goals around them and celebrate their accomplishments and improvements.

- **Annual turnover rate**. The number of employees who have left the center, divided by the number of total employees.
- **Sick time usage**. Hours used annually by center staff.
- **Trainee success rate**. The number of trainees who graduated the hiring phase, divided by the total number of hired during that phase.
- **Trainee retention rate**. The number of trainees still employed after three years divided by total number hired in group.
- **9-1-1 answer rate**. Percentage of calls answered within minimum APCO, NENA, NFPA, or other nationally accredited standard.
- **Substantiated citizen complaints**. Quantity of sustained complaints in the current year.
- **Dispatch time for PD, Fire, EMS**. Number of seconds it takes from call answer to call dispatch.
- **QA checks**. Averaged compliance score.
- **Training hours**. The number of hours of training each year per employee.
- **NCIC message volume**. By employee, per shift.

Tracking each of these metrics allows you to quantify your specific center's situation. These are key performance indicators, or KPIs, that tell a part of the story. Some centers report having no problem with turnover. In fact, they wish some of their people would leave (there's definitely such a thing as *positive* turnover). These same centers, however, have a huge problem with sick time abuse and long dispatch times. We have to look at the entire picture to understand the truth.

Self-Assessment

1. Where is your center with regard to your metrics? The numbers don't lie.
2. If you aren't tracking your numbers regularly, which technology solution does your center use that can help with this?
3. How can you improve your metrics to bring them more in line with industry best practices?

You can access the full list industry standards and best practices online. APCO (www.apco.org), NENA (www.nena.org), International Academies of Emergency Dispatch (www.emergencydispatch.org) and National Fire Protection Association (www.nfpa.org) all provide sections on downloadable industry standards.

CHAPTER 12

MAKE YOUR CULTURE WORK FOR YOU

When I ask a manager or supervisor what they see as their center's biggest challenge—the one thing that, if it were to change, would make the biggest positive difference on the center's day-to-day operations—I often hear, "The culture. If we could improve the culture, then we'd be in a much better place."

While it's true that a positive culture will produce better results, the more important question is, "How are you going to do that?" Because "culture" isn't a singular thing. As first discussed in Chapter 5, it's not a single challenge, like coming into work on time, that can be discussed, documented, remediated, and reviewed. It's not black and white. Culture is the sum of many different variables, all of them important.

That doesn't mean it *can't* change, or that we should stop trying. It just means we have to know what we really mean when we say we're going to do it and realize that there's no short-term fix. Culture takes years to develop. Short-term problems often trigger a fear response because a reflex action might fix them, whereas deep, evident structural problems cause people to step back and process sensibly because no amount of hysteria can fix them. Consider the saying, "You would be tempted to jump a 15-foot gap, but you would look for an entirely different way to cross a 100-yard chasm."

The problem is, one may be tempted to claim they don't really *need* to make these changes. Employees will still do the work, answer calls, and dispatch officers, even if we have a bad culture that drives people out of the organization. We can always mandate OT when there are no volunteers. That's why it takes courage to meet this unique challenge proactively, head-on.

If you do not address the behaviors that lead to a negative culture, it is impossible to effectively transition to the new. There are ways to cross this 100-yard chasm:

1. **Work with and within your current culture.** You won't change or replace culture by posting inspirational phrases on the walls or by assigning mandatory reading. Even major overhaul efforts may fall short. It's important, then, to understand the dynamics of your center's culture, and to realize it's not all bad. Note which aspects of your culture may be preventing your center from being successful and which are a part of your success.

   For example, I often hear from centers that when the team is working an urgent, life-threatening call or field situation, they appreciate the teamwork and support that arises during these emergency situations. One center decided to use the example set by their team's response to emergencies as a model for how they'd like to feel supported during non-emergency operations. By talking about the behaviors they'd like to see more of versus those they wanted to see less of and holding each other accountable for behaving in the new way, the culture began to shift.

2. **Change behaviors, and mindsets will follow.** It's tempting to believe that behavior shifts follow mindset shifts, which is why many organizational change efforts begin with doing some work around core values, and then posting these on the wall. The problem with this is that the values posted on the wall means different things to different people, and habits are hard to break, so the shiny new values statement will do little to correct faulty behaviors until more work is done.

It wasn't until Grand Junction RECC, from Chapter 7, translated their new values statement into clearly defined "in-bounds" and "out-of-bounds" behavior that things began to change. They also had to decide on new practices for interpersonal communication, in order to begin holding each other accountable to the agreed-upon behavioral shifts in a mutually respectful way. Each member of the team was part of the behavior change and agreed to empower each other to uphold peer-to-peer accountability.

3. **Focus on a few critical behaviors.** The tendency is to think we need to change everything—all at once. Instead, it's much more beneficial and easier to focus on a few critical behaviors that will make a pronounced difference. Once you've decided on the behaviors, translate them into simple, practical steps that people can take every day.

   One comm center did this by focusing on the way supervisors communicated with employees, changing how disciplinary action was handled and creating consistency across the supervisory team. Instead of telling employees what they did wrong, supervisors began having coaching conversations. With discipline, supervisors had a tendency to play "whack-a-mole," writing people up for small things and big things alike. To change this, they began asking questions and engaging people, using formal discipline only as a last resort. To create consistency across teams, supervisors were trained on how to communicate, and they began meeting regularly. Instead of four supervisors doing things in four different ways, they began functioning as a cohesive team.

4. **Deploy your informal leaders.** Positional power and authority, conferred by job title and rank, should not be confused with leadership. Leadership is a natural attribute, exercised and displayed informally without regard to title or position. We've discussed how every center also has informal leaders but are often not recognized as such. As a result, they

are frequently overlooked and underused when it comes to driving culture. They can become powerful allies who can influence behavior through "showing by doing."

5. **Don't let your formal leaders off the hook.** It can be tempting to push the change initiative onto the front line supervisors or middle management, but leaders in all parts of the organization are critical to the effort. If employees see a disconnect between the culture an organization claims to uphold and the one its highest level of formal leadership actually follows, they'll disengage quickly from the advertised culture and simply mimic the higher-ups. The people at the top have to demonstrate the change they want to see.

   At the comm center, it's tempting to think that an absentee manager, director, sergeant or lieutenant doesn't *really* have influence on center culture. They don't always (or ever) participate in day-to-day operations, after all. It was years before the police chief at one center in Texas took notice of the sergeant's effect on communications' morale. During that 9-year run, the sergeant didn't interact with the staff, didn't pay attention to their concerns, and largely left the training coordinator to be the staff liaison. This in itself wouldn't have been a problem if the training coordinator had been sufficiently empowered to make operational decisions. Instead, the sergeant remained disconnected and non-observant until, after a vote of "no confidence" facilitated by an outside consultant, the chief informed the sergeant that his services would no longer be needed. Thankfully, the incoming sergeant has been a force for positive change.

6. **Link behaviors to center goals and objectives.** When people talk about feelings, motivations and values—all of which are vital elements of strong cultures—the conversation can often veer into the abstract. It may

then feel like an intangible discussion that ends up confusing things. Too many employees walk away from culture-focused meetings or values discussions wondering how the advice on how to be a better person actually translates into the work they do. To avoid such a disconnect, offer tangible, well-defined examples of how cultural interventions lead to improved performance and clear results.

When the team at Sugar Land Public Safety Dispatch saw an opportunity to improve their trainee success rate, they decided to approach it in a whole new way. The annual turnover rate had been consistently dropping, while the trainee success rate sat at a steady 50% during the same time. The Director, Training Coordinator and CTOs met and decided on specific changes to the training program. One change included placing the responsibility for the trainees' success onto the CTO. Holding the CTOs accountable for their trainees' success changed the way the CTOs thought about their role as instructor. The CTOs decided they needed to meet with their trainees off the floor more frequently and take the time to coach and guide the trainees through the process.

Prior to this meeting, CTOs would meet with their trainees once a month, discussing improvement points and course corrective behaviors. The problem was, after 30 days, the trainees' bad habits were sometimes already firmly entrenched, making corrective action more difficult. Seeing this, the CTOs decided to begin having these check-in meetings once a week. Within a year, trainee success had increased to 80%.

7. **Demonstrate impact quickly.** We live in an age of notoriously short attention spans. That applies as much to organizational culture as it does to people's media consumption habits. When people hear about the changes that are going to take place but don't see any activity related to them for several months, they'll disengage and grow cynical. It's

extremely important to showcase the impact of cultural efforts on center performance results as quickly as possible.

More than one director I interviewed for this book explained the swift action they took relative to the changes they were brought on to make. One director said, "Within a month, I had flipped the place upside down." Another said, "It was within weeks into my new position that I had found money for new chairs and consoles, and this was just the start. The team members said it was the first time that anyone had gone to bat for them." Another director spent his first week on the job meeting with all 145 employees, giving them time to share their concerns surrounding the upcoming changes. Once real results are demonstrated, the next step is to keep going.

8. **Use cross-organizational methods to bring the team together.** Ideas can spread virally across shifts and teams, as well as from the top down and bottom up. One powerful way to spread ideas is through email and social media, such as blogs, Facebook posts and tweets—not from upper management but from the informal leaders we talked about above. It's well established that online methods can be more effective at spreading information, news, and music than traditional modes of distribution. The same holds with critical behaviors. People are often more receptive to changes in "the way we do things around here" when friends, colleagues, and other peers share and recommend those changes.

In a 24-hour business like 9-1-1, it's easy for certain shifts or watches to lose touch with the rest of the organization. Organization-wide communication can help overcome this challenge. Many centers have experimented with weekly or monthly newsletters that feature stories of lives saved, work anniversaries, birthdays, or other accomplishments, only to have the effort abandoned because the daily workload got "too busy." If you can connect these announcements and information shares to the critical behavior shifts needed for deep and lasting change, you'll encourage people to prioritize the time required to keep these initiatives going. If these methods are complementary to the larger mission, they're less likely to be abandoned down the road. More than one center uses their social media presence to make sure everyone is on the same page, both with regard to things happening in their community and at the center.

9. **Align the formal structure with behaviors.** While informal leaders can help change culture from within and make ideas go viral, it's important to match the new cultural direction with existing ways of working. Informal mechanisms and cultural interventions must complement and integrate with the more common formal organization components, not work against them. By providing the structure in which people work—through disciplines such as organization design, data analysis, human resources, and process improvement—the formal organization provides a rational motivation for employee actions, while the informal organization enables the emotional commitment that characterizes peak performance.

   A director at a comm center in Illinois saw that the number of employees had grown over time beyond the point where he could continue to be the director, supervisor and training manager, all at once. His span of control had grown too large and was causing many in the organization to feel alienated. In an effort to improve morale and to increase employee engagement, he got approval to create three supervisor spots (one for each watch), along with an operations manager position. At a certain point, there is simply too much work for one person to be the only level of management at a comm center.

10. **Actively manage your cultural situation over time.** Centers that maintain a positive culture actively monitor, manage, care for, and update their cultural forces. When aligned with operational priorities, culture can

provide hidden sources of energy and motivation that can accelerate changes faster than formal processes and programs. Even today's highly effective culture may not be good enough for tomorrow.

The best centers are never "done" working on creating a culture conducive to their success. We work in an ever-changing industry with high turnover; if your center doesn't regularly repeat the process above, impressive gains can be lost when a key employee departs the organization. In 2005, a California comm center providing police, fire & EMS services reported a 1% turnover rate after six years of trying different methods to improve the organization. At the time of this writing (2018), their turnover rate has returned to the 20%+ rate they had prior to the organizational initiatives used to keep their best people. When the managers who oversaw the pre-2005 change initiative left the organization, the knowledge also left. With no one to guide the culture and the initiatives that led to its evolution, it returned to its default state.

To a degree, culture can be compared to natural forces such as winds and tides. These elements are there in the background—sometimes unnoticed, sometimes obvious. Endowed with immense power, they can waylay plans and inhibit progress. You can't really tame or fundamentally alter them. But if you respect them and understand how to make the most of them—if you work with them and tap their hidden power—they can become a source of energy and provide powerful assistance.

The best way to start is to ask yourself a series of questions. What are the most important emotional forces that determine what your people do? What few behavior changes would matter most in meeting operational imperatives? Who are the informal leaders you can enlist? What can you and others at your level of the organization do differently to signal and reinforce those critical behaviors?

Of course, you shouldn't plan for dramatic results overnight. Expect an evolution, not a revolution. One of the challenges of working with culture is that it changes gradually. That's the bad news. The good news? If you approach culture with respect and intelligence, you can use it to differentiate your center and to help the work get done more easily.

THE CHANGE AGENTS

Today, right now, *at this moment*, there are change agents at your center who can be a part of establishing your center's new approach. Again, you cannot try or hope to do it alone. Part of enlisting informal leaders' help is that they will help make the changes more palatable to the majority, who is likely going to be resistant to any change—even the positive kind.

Be on the lookout for these change agents as you talk to your people. These are the team members who have ideas, make suggestions, and seem willing to put their ideas out there. Asking open-ended questions about where the organization could go and how to get there will offer an opportunity to solicit feedback. It can also help gauge where people are with regard to their thinking and how receptive they are to possible changes. When you've found a potential change agent, make a note: what are they passionate about? Where do their skills and interests lie? Do they have a track record of success? Are they well-liked at the center?

Once you've identified this individual, think about how to sell the idea of being on a development team in terms that matter to them. For instance, the culture you're trying to change might include a dimension of deep distrust towards the higher-ups or management. This person may fear being seen by the rest at the comm center as having crossed over to the dark side of the hated supervisors, in which case they'll decline the request, even if they're initially interested. The power of peer pressure is strong. If, instead, you've identified a person who is dedicated to being a part of something that will benefit everyone, and if you have tailored your invitation to highlight the fit for that individual, you're more likely to get a yes from this great candidate.

Pushing the initiative down to the front line employees as much and as often as you can fosters buy-in and inclusion in the process. This regulates the fear of change and promotes teamwork during what could prove to be a challenging time. By prioritizing buy-in and inclusion—especially during a change initiative—the team realizes they did something challenging together that they couldn't have accomplished without one another. This energy carries further into whatever follows. As change builds momentum and the team sees what else is possible, more actually *becomes* possible.

Self-Assessment

Your center's culture is either helping or hindering success.

1. Who are your formal and informal leaders who can be a part of the culture change?
2. If you haven't identified your informal leaders, how might you do this? How can you help them join your efforts in getting others on board?
3. How will you quantify and measure the shift?

CHAPTER 13
WITHOUT ACCOUNTABILITY, THERE IS NO STANDARD

As discussed in Chapter 10, integrity is essential for building trust, but it doesn't work unless it's paired with accountability. Accountability is the glue that holds your transition together. It is the only way to connect your teams and to have them function on the same page. To embrace accountability, we must be willing to communicate during tough times and to embrace radical transparency.

In the 1960s, workplace and behavioral psychologist John Stacey Adams asserted that employees seek to maintain equity between the effort they expend at their job and what they get from it, against how they perceive other employees' inputs and outcomes.

In short, people value fair treatment; this motivates them to keep the fairness maintained within the relationships of their coworkers and the organization. Said in another way, if employees perceive inequity (or unfairness), they will seek to reduce it, either by distorting inputs and/or outcomes in their own minds (cognitive distortion), directly altering inputs and/or outcomes, or leaving the organization.

Chapter 8 talked a bit about how the power of any change initiative can only be unleashed when a high degree of trust exists. Accountability is the foundation of trust. Invariably, promises made will be broken and expectations violated. Holding each other accountable for actions taken (or not taken) is the only way to make a change. In order to hold each other accountable, it's necessary to clearly state the expectations.

In the book *Crucial Accountability*, the authors put it like this:

> You can't solve longstanding problems if you haven't let others know exactly what you want. With unclear expectations, you don't have the right to hold others accountable to violations they may not be aware of. Confront the past. Without singling anyone out, outline for people the natural consequences of how things have been. For example, you may describe how the habit of treating others disrespectfully has created a negative work environment the causes employees to quit and call in sick. As you help people connect consequences with past behavior, you build moral authority for resetting expectations.
>
> Illuminate your general vision of how things are going to be in the future with specific, identifiable, and replicable actions. Clarify dos and don'ts. Study best practices. Contrast what people used to do with what they need to do now. Then teach and focus on those specific actions. If you don't know precisely what you're looking for, you have no right to expect it. Only after you've clarified your new expectation do you have the right to begin having accountability conversations with those who violate the new standards. More than a right, it will then be a responsibility.

What does it look like to clarify expectations and hold each other accountable like this at the comm center? It starts with the vision. If the vision is to have a high-performing comm center—one where people like to work, have fun while doing it, and work with a high level of professionalism—this vision will inform the mission statement and core values. Once you have your core values, you can begin fleshing them out into actionable behaviors—the same way Grand Junction RECC specifically stated "in-bounds" and "out-of-bounds" behavior. The in-bounds behavior becomes the cause of positive reinforcement through praise and recognition, while the out-of-bounds behavior prompts accountability conversations.

An accountability conversation can only take place when there's been a violation of an explicitly stated expectation. The problem often experienced in the comm center is that no one communicates any expectations, so anything will suffice. Worse yet, we claim that mutual respect is important; but no one says or does anything when a coworker speaks in a clearly derogatory tone or a supervisor snaps at a direct report. None of us would agree to work in a hostile work environment, yet many of contribute to the hostility on a regular basis.

Once the expectations are clear and everyone has agreed to uphold them, they serve as the stable foundation for accountability conversations, if violated.

WORKING WITH VIOLATED EXPECTATIONS

The first step in holding coworkers (peers, direct reports, higher-ups) accountable is to understand the stories you tell when a commitment has been violated. The story you tell about the other person flows directly into the feelings you have about the situation, which influences what you say. The authors of the book *Crucial Conversations* offer this model:

A coworker violates a commitment, and we're propelled into action. We see what the person did, and then we tell ourselves a story about why he or she did it, which leads to a feeling, which lead to our own action. If the story is unflattering and the feeling is anger, adrenaline kicks in. Under the influence of adrenaline, blood leaves our brains to help support the fight-or-flight response, and we end up thinking with our limbic brain. We say and do dumb things. When we're always stuck in this negative thinking loop—always telling unflattering stories about the citizens, officer, coworkers, family members, etc.—we may find ourselves stuck in this reptilian state of thinking.

The story you tell about your coworker, especially when they've violated an expectation, almost always involves a *fundamental attribution* error. This describes our tendency to attribute a person's actions to who they are, instead of a single mistake. We are very bad at understanding the motivation or situation behind people's actions; we instead blame them for being "stupid" or "lazy." But so often, their actions are a result of a specific and temporary situation: the man riding the bus with his three small children who are running around all over the place creating a ruckus is traveling from his wife's funeral. The caller reporting the loud music at 11pm that woke her baby up has never called the police before.

When we attribute a singular mistake to a person's very nature, we're probably wrong. With a tainted history between you and that person, the likelihood that you *are* wrong increases, and the effects of the story you tell becomes more severe. If you frequently "tell people like it is" in a rude or condescending tone because "they had it coming," there may be a different story to tell that might get you better results. But how do you challenge your story, especially when it feels so right? What does it take to avoid making the fundamental attribution error, becoming angry, and then establishing a hostile climate? We have to tell the rest of the story.

Since the problem of coming up with ugly stories and suffering the consequences takes place within the confines of your own mind, that's where the solution lies as well. Instead of talking yourself into a fervor after observing a violated expectation with a question like, *"What's wrong with that person?!"* you can instead ask a humanizing question like, "Why would a reasonable, rational, and decent person do that?" This second question allows you to begin to bridge the divide that exists between you and the other person. You can see them as another human, with similar concerns, challenges, and desires.

When you don't humanize the violator, it's too easy to fall into the attribution error—to simply see them as "another stupid person who just doesn't get it," instead of a reasonable and rational person who either didn't understand the expectation, is having a bad day, or didn't intentionally violate the expectation. The problem is that most times, when an expectation is violated, we just let it go without venturing into a conversation that could illuminate the real reason for what happened. We forgo the opportunity to build connection, understand another's viewpoint, and improve the possibility of a healthy working relationship.

Or at least we *pretend* to let it go. But we frequently don't. We make a mental note about that person and their violation, and we hold on to it. We brood about it, we tell others, and it festers. A few days or a few weeks later, that infraction—no matter how small or big—has become exponentially worse in our own minds.

These (usually small) infractions don't cause everyone in the comm center hate each other. The culprit is our unwillingness to talk about things we'd rather not talk about. Team members at the best centers have the courage to venture into these conversations.

NO ACCOUNTABILITY, NO TEAM

If we're unwilling (or unable) to undertake accountability conversations when expectations are violated, we shouldn't be surprised to find that everyone treats everyone however they feel like treating people in that moment. If I'm tired and cranky, *you better watch out!* If I'm feeling good because I slept well and had my coffee, please feel free to approach.

The exemplary centers that have become places where people *want* to work—instead of simply tolerating because finding another job is a hassle—have found the courage to redefine what it means to be a part of a highly-functioning team. The norm is to say, "They're a good dispatcher. They're great at the job—I'd trust them working a console on any shift during any situation—but they sure aren't very nice. In fact, they're one of the crustiest employees we have here." The exemplary centers dare to say, "You're not a 'good' dispatcher if you're not both good at the job *and* work well with others. We spend way too much time together to be at each other's throats."

The vehicle by which a center maintains this standard is accountability. If someone violates a core value, any policy, or otherwise infringes upon the expectations everyone in the center has agreed to live by, it must be grounds for a conversation. If you're unwilling to have conversations to hold people accountable, this is an important realization to dissect and understand. Is it because of a fear of confrontation? Is it because of a lack of skill in engaging in this type of conversation? Does it depend on the situation? As with emotional intelligence, the first step is self-awareness.

There's a lot of talk about how much of this responsibility falls on the shoulders of leadership. A supervisor in one of my leadership sessions at a conference spoke to this exactly. "You know," she proclaimed, "it sounds like you're blaming a lot of what goes wrong at the comm center on the supervisory team. I don't think that's fair." Fair or not, if supervisors aren't willing to have tough conversations, then there's no way the front line employees are going to hold each other accountable. Everyone is looking to everyone else for the acceptable practice. Unfortunately for many comm centers, people are more focused on what they can get away with than how they can make their center a better place to work. It's center management's responsibility to model the expected behavior.

What if I—as a mid-level supervisor or lead—don't see the manager/director/chief or whoever else is "in charge" all that frequently? Then it's incumbent upon the leaders in the room to hold people accountable. What if I try holding someone accountable, and they say, "You're not the boss!" so they keep committing the questionable behavior? When someone goes on the offense to defend behavior that's in clear violation of the expectation the team has set forth, mention that. What if we don't have core values or a code of conduct or clear policies that dictate how we'd like to be treated and how to treat each other? Start there, in whatever way you can. Instead of saying, "Someone should really do something about this," try *being* that someone.

Once you've implemented the beginnings of a turnaround, next comes the work of sustaining the change.

This part can be tricky. I have discovered in my time as a turnaround consultant that initial change can actually be the relatively easy part. Many of the centers I consult with are excited about change but find that turnarounds can lose steam as people and centers settle back into their day-to-day habits, routines and patterns. In the next section, I discuss how to avoid doing so and how to hold on to your hard-earned results.

Self-Assessment

1. Where could your center do better at holding each other accountable?
2. What accountability conversation(s) are you delaying?
3. What's preventing you from having this necessary conversation?

In several case studies for this book, the change initiative began with sending the leadership team to a training class that taught effective communication skills. Knowing how to say the right thing increases the likelihood that an accountability conversation can and will take place.

PART THREE:

SUSTAINING THE CHANGE

CHAPTER 14

GETTING THE RIGHT PEOPLE IN THE SEATS

To sustain success over the long-term, it takes constant work. As the stories throughout this book attest, even the results of the most heroic positive change initiative can fall by the wayside after a few years. Offered as a cautionary tale, these stories point the way towards building a center that thrives year after year after year—and keeps going.

It's no mistake that the word "success" is contained within "succession planning." Sustaining success of a change initiative takes a marathon mindset, and the willingness to constantly reinvent, should the ongoing evaluation of your operation yield new information. If we commit to quality through continuous improvement, then we know the work is never done.

RECRUITING AND HIRING THE RIGHT PEOPLE

While the quest to hire the right people is never-ending, it doesn't have to be a fruitless journey. The best centers have dared to re-engineer the hiring and recruitment process after facing the facts: our system is broken. Many saw one or more indicators that their hiring and recruitment process was malfunctioning:

- Waiting to begin the recruitment process until you really "need" people
- New hires resigning because they didn't know what they were getting into
- Not offering ride-alongs/sit-alongs during the recruitment process

- Not involving the candidate's family in the process, allowing them to ask questions
- Hiring candidates based on the "hoped for" fit
- Not using CritiCall or some other early skills testing/ evaluation method
- Background investigation is unnecessarily intrusive
- Communications section has no input during interview process
- Selection process is a subjective vote by shifts or watches instead of being an objective, criteria-based process

Addressing each one of these indicators will increase the likelihood that your new people stick around and succeed in their new role. It's not easy to attract and hire the right people, but it's even more unfortunate when we *don't know* if we're hiring the right people. Here's how a few agencies have overcome each of these challenges.

Waiting to begin the recruitment process until you really "need" people

In 2001, Santa Cruz Police Communications sat at a turnover rate higher than the national average despite years of trying everything to improve their numbers. They had tried throwing money at the problem, building a new center with natural light and a beautiful view of the adjacent forest. They reorganized the center's management structure. They bought brand-new consoles and chairs. They raised pay rates by 18.1%.

The turnover rate remained unchanged despite all of the above enhancements.

They kept at it. They continued to innovate, trying different things. Over the next four years, they implemented a series of changes that eventually drove turnover down to less than one percent. One of the methods they used was deploying four "unfunded overhire" positions. In the event someone quit, they would have a trained person ready to step into the role. They also made adjustments to their lateral transfer policy and implemented a 3-year recruitment and retention plan. This plan resulted in three dispatch academies in a one-year period through continuous hiring. To get candidates for all the academies that year, they deployed a recruitment team and a citizens' academy, revisited test score cut-offs, moved the background screening to the front of process, and used a peer review process. In short, they learned that having good people in place before they "needed" them ensured they'd have the right people when they did.

New hires resigning because they didn't know what they were getting into

The best centers know that every part of the hiring process is an opportunity to inform a candidate about the job. Beginning with the job posting until the formal job offer, each step must accurately portray the rigors and rewards of a career in 9-1-1. A lot of 9-1-1 job postings are unnaturally rosy, painting a picture of all the pluses and none of the challenges. Many agencies require a candidate to spend a few hours in the comm center observing. However, I disagree with the practice of evaluating the candidate during the sit-along and weighting this evaluation against the rest of the hiring process. Especially in centers with a darkly cynical culture, these evaluations are overly critical at best and wildly inaccurate at worst.

During the sit-along, the candidate should have an opportunity to ask questions and hear about the job from a true perspective. Choosing the right person with whom to pair a prospective candidate is also important. If you'd like the person to want to continue in the process, pairing them with the known bully in the center is probably not the best approach.

Further along in the process, one Colorado center invites the candidate's family to a meeting attended by the center's manager and supervisor. The family is invited to ask questions about the job, and they are told to expect their family member to be working days, nights, weekends, holidays, and whenever else required to do so. Not surprisingly, this particular center places a strong emphasis on family, both in and out of the center, and it has strongly inclusive culture as a result.

While some individuals simply can't do this job—and unfortunately won't show this until they're in the training process—screening them out by giving them a sober understanding of what the job entails prevents them from misreading the situation. It also prevents the agency from spending any more time, attention, and money on someone who isn't a good fit.

Not offering ride-alongs / sit-alongs

Giving candidates an opportunity to get a real feel for the work does wonders. They can see what the work entails, have a conversation with their potential future coworkers, and learn much more than reading the job description could ever impart. If your center's culture is negative and populated with a few toxic bullies, they will drive away good candidates. This comes back to the need to have an accountability conversation to change this behavior *before* you hire any more people.

Hiring candidates based on the "hoped for" fit

Several center managers explained their challenges related to optimistic thinking during the hiring process. They shared stories of candidates putting their best foot forward, getting the job offer, and then not working out because they weren't the right fit for the center *culture.* This goes back to the "feeling" side of organizational life. You can have a candidate with 9-1-1 experience and who can perform the mechanics of the job well but isn't kind and compassionate with callers or coworkers. If kindness and respect towards people are values that matter to your center's culture, and your recruitment and hiring process doesn't have anything geared towards screening for these qualities, there's an opportunity waiting.

One director said me, "I can teach someone the skills of the job; I can't teach them to be nice. We don't have the time to teach compassion with everything else we've got going on. We hire for fit NOW, not for what we hope the person will become during training." Remarkably, this center has placed more of an emphasis on hiring people from a customer service background, finding that those with a 9-1-1 background were already steeped in the negativity that this center prides itself on avoiding. CritiCall or some other early skills testing/evaluation method can also help ensure this fit from the outset, instead of later in the process, which leads to our next point.

Not using CritiCall or some other early skills testing/evaluation method

Similar to offering sit-alongs, early skills testing gives candidates (and the center) an opportunity to set expectations and to gauge fit before the job offer. A good training program can get a skilled candidate up to speed, but if you don't test for a baseline level of skills, how can you know what you're getting? Some agencies forego using such a service because of the cost. But the true cost associated with hiring someone who never could learn the job, burning out the instructor, and then going back to the hiring board is much greater.

Background investigation is unnecessarily intrusive

In the not-too-distant past, one center's background investigation employed the services of a private investigator. The P.I. would visit a prospective candidate's home, and while there, ask the candidate to sign in to their private Facebook account so the P.I. could inspect the contents of recent posts. When the new director discovered this practice, he quickly disbanded it, seeing that it was a product of the past director's management style of power and control.

At LAPD, civilian employees (dispatchers included), only sat with a background investigator for a brief interview to go over gaps of employment offered on the application and to answer questions regarding drug use. No home visit or polygraph was administered. Many agencies apply the same rules for background to civilian and sworn. Some agencies approach it entirely differently. Often left untouched as "the way it's always been done," even background investigation protocol must be changed if it prevents your center from gaining good candidates.

Communications has no input during interview process

Whoever handles hiring for your agency—city personnel, county HR, or the like—must give Communications a hands-on role at some point in the process, or there's an opportunity. Only those who work under the headset can ask the pertinent questions and vet the answers according to their real-world application. Centers across the country, including several I spoke with for this book, have dramatically improved their candidate fit and training program success by giving Communications personnel a seat on the interview board, or somewhere else in the screening process. One center went from a "hire everyone who meets the bare minimum" hiring philosophy to re-engineering the oral interview process by asking pointed, values-driven, culture-related questions.

Selection is a subjective vote by watches instead of an objective, criteria-based process

Similar to the note above regarding sit-alongs, the employees of a center with a pervasively negative culture are not impartial. In some ways, their rejection of prospective candidates is an affront to current management, whom they view as the source of their frustration. Further, if current employees don't believe in the hiring, recruitment, selection, and training process, they view all of it through a tainted filter. It's still important to get employee buy-in for hiring decisions at a center like this. However, protecting candidates from the wrath of the caustically negative, and taking measures to prevent the selection process from being swayed by this disposition, can help keep good candidates around while the change initiative is still unfolding. Typically, just 10% of your total roster will be of the actively disengaged, angry type. Schedule your sit-alongs and trainings to avoid these bad eggs.

Self-Assessment

1. Take a look at your recruitment and hiring approach. Where do you see opportunities to do better? Are you making any of the mistakes outlined in this chapter?
2. How can you better shape people's expectations of the job so they aren't surprised by the apparent and immediate challenges the job poses?

CHAPTER 15

MANAGE PERFORMANCE WITH FEEDBACK

Continually hiring the right people gets them *in* the door; giving regular feedback on their performance keeps them engaged and on the path of excellence. Once someone is in the job, works it for two to three years and can do it in their sleep, their biggest enemy is stagnation. Too often, telecommunicators are left to take call after call, shift after shift, without getting any feedback as to what they could be doing better or how they're doing at all. Not being able to objectively measure the quality of one's work is one of the signs of a miserable job that author Patrick Lencioni shares in his book *The Three Signs of a Miserable Job*. In fact, one recent study found that those who didn't get feedback were no better off than those who received negative feedback.

In Daniel Pink's book *Drive: The Surprising Truth About What Motivates Us*, he outlines the driving forces that animate our daily work. When these forces are present, motivation is available. When they aren't, anything can feel like drudgery. One of these forces is mastery. People are driven by the knowledge that they are getting better at things, improving, and approaching mastery.

There is always room for improvement in 9-1-1. We can communicate better (with citizens and our coworkers); we can be better leaders; we can be more compassionate. Becoming better at these things translates into being better adapting to change and rolling with the inevitable challenges of life. We become masters of adeptly rolling with the punches.

Without measuring our advancement towards becoming a better calltaker, dispatcher, or supervisor, we begin to wonder what the point is. Then, when we're forced to work OT, cover a holiday or get bumped to graveyards, it's a lot more difficult to answer the question, "What am I working so hard for?"

Lisa had been a telecommunicator for about 3 years when she hit a wall. Despite knowing her work was meaningful (she was saving lives, after all), she couldn't shake the feeling she could be doing more with her life. The fact that she frequently worked overtime could've been a factor, but she and her family appreciated the larger paycheck. Her coworkers were sometimes a challenge to deal with, but for the most part, she got along with everyone. Then another consideration dawned on her.

Ever since she'd gotten out of training, Lisa never really knew if she was doing a good job. The few times she'd received feedback from her supervisor, it was negative. In one instance, it was constructive to know she'd made a mistake while creating the call, but the way her manager offered the criticism was pretty rough. The general feeling among employees at the center was, "You better not screw up, or you'll get in trouble." Fear permeated the organization. There was a lot of gossip and a strong rumor mill.

Lisa's experience is not unique. Little feedback, poor communication, and a lack of empathy seem to be the norm, and not just at 9-1-1 comm centers. Such challenges persist in many organizations across a wide variety of industries. Leaders at exceptional workplaces, however, choose to use a better way. By exploring this better way of communicating feedback and adjusting our approach accordingly, we can make certain that dedicated team members excel in a job they find challenging yet deeply meaningful.

Giving team members regular feedback is essential for a number of reasons. It provides an opportunity for them to course-correct if they're not doing so well. When dispensed weekly, it gives supervisors a perfect avenue for building rapport and trust while offering the chance to catch employees doing something right. One director requires his supervisors to maintain a positive-to-negative feedback ratio of 3 to 1. This is much easier to do when giving feedback is built into the workweek.

The problem is, feedback doesn't work in most organizations. A glance at the stats from the general corporate world tells the story: only 36% of supervisors complete appraisals thoroughly and on time. In one recent survey, 55% of employees said their most recent performance review had been unfair or inaccurate, and one in four said they dread such evaluations more than anything else in their working lives. Part of the problem is caused by the supervisor's inability or unwillingness to have difficult feedback discussions.

In addition to an inability or unwillingness to wade into these difficult yet necessary feedback discussions, there's the tone that supervisors use when dispensing most feedback. When an employee makes a mistake, the natural response is frustration, especially if the mistake reflects poorly on the agency or has the potential to put officer or citizen safety at risk. The traditional approach is to reprimand the employee in some way, in the hope that the punishment will be beneficial. By "teaching them a lesson," we hope they won't do it again.

However, the research says that a more compassionate response gets better results. First, compassion and curiosity increase employee loyalty and trust. Research has shown that feelings of warmth and positive relationships at work have a greater say over an employee's loyalty than the size of his or her paycheck. Conversely, responding with anger or frustration erodes loyalty. If you embarrass or blame an employee too harshly, your reaction may end up coming around to haunt you. "Next time you need to rely on that employee, you may have lost some of the loyalty that was there before," says Adam Grant, professor at the Wharton Business School and author of *Give and Take.*

We are especially sensitive to signs of trustworthiness in our leaders, and compassion increases our willingness to trust. Simply put, our brains respond more positively to bosses who have shown us empathy. Employee trust in turn improves performance.

This is part of the reason why comm center leaders who prioritize building relationships with their people are able to inspire positive change more effectively than managers who do not. These exemplary leaders use even the most challenging moments of discussion to build the employee up, instead of tearing them down.

Aside from examining your personal approach to dispensing feedback, the best centers have organizational structures, policies and systems in place that ensure the opportunity to give regular feedback isn't merely left to chance.

THE POWER OF A QA APPROACH

One recommendation I have for my consulting clients is to implement and correctly use a powerful QA approach. While many centers have some sort of QA procedure, I've found that many fail to use QA to its full potential.

In 2015, APCO & NENA released their *Standard for Establishment of a Quality Assurance and Quality Improvement (QA/QI) Program at Public Safety Answering Points*. The standard emerged from a demonstrated need for a consistently applied protocol of telecommunicator call-handling performance and improvement. One of the authors and major proponents of the standard was Nathan Lee, husband to Denise Amber Lee, who was slain after a failure of the 9-1-1 system in the area of her residence.

Denise was abducted from the Lees' rented home in North Port, Florida, in the middle of the day. Somehow, the intruder gained entry and control of Denise, who most likely saved her children's lives. Denise's father, Detective Rick Goff, was able to call all area state, county and municipal law-enforcement agencies to search for Denise and her captor immediately following her abduction. It was one of the most massive, cooperative search efforts this area ever experienced.

In the hours that ensued, Denise fought mightily for her life. In her battle, she was able to use the captor's cell phone to call 9-1-1, an act she thought would save her life—just like all of us are taught as children. She was not the only one to call 9-1-1 that day regarding this crime. There were at least four other calls, one from her distraught husband and three from eyewitnesses. One witness gave the local sheriff's department an exact location of the crime happening right before her eyes. She stayed on the phone for more than nine minutes, identifying cross streets as she continued driving. As many as four patrol cars were within a mile of the car in which Denise was fighting for her life, but due to inefficiencies in the call center, none were dispatched. On the morning of January 19, 2008, two heart-wrenching days after she went missing, Denise Lee's body was found.

This breakdown in the 9-1-1 system was not a technical breakdown. All the calls placed were connected. The phones and CAD systems worked that day. Rather, it was a breakdown in adherence to protocol and to proactive supervision leading up to that day. Quality assurance and quality improvement (QA/QI) programs are designed and implemented in the hopes that they help *prevent* something like this from happening. If the complacency that resulted in Denise's loss of life can be prevented from doing regular QA, is it not worth its regular use?

Unfortunately, quality assurance and quality improvement programs frequently get a bad rap due to the way they are rolled out. Since the front line receives mostly negative feedback, they're likely to perceive any effort management makes to offer *more* feedback with suspicion. I've heard many comm center employees say, "They're just trying to get us into trouble."

Communication is important here, as a matter of framing the QA program in a positive light. Sure, call monitoring sometimes catches people in a lapse of judgement or doing questionable things. But this isn't the point of the program. The goal is to catch people doing great work, while ensuring the quality of total work output. If tied back to the center's core values, it's a powerful way to keep looping back to what your center stands for. If one of your core values is "Excellence in all we say and do," for example, the QA program is one of the best opportunities center supervision has for maintaining a consistent standard of excellence.

Oftentimes, however, there is no communication surrounding the implementation of a QA program. No one gives any context about why it's so important and the opportunity it provides for the center. Rather, it's unceremoniously thrust upon center staff as just *another* required duty. The best centers view QA and every new system, policy, procedure, or process implementation as a chance to reinforce their commitment to being an exemplary center. They frame it this way from the earliest stages, throughout the rollout, and during its use.

When used to its fullest potential, a QA program offers the structure and excuse for center leadership to provide weekly coaching and performance feedback for employees. Said in another way, it's a chance to build connection and provide guidance. An employee who works at a center where they abandoned their proactive QA practices due to low staffing levels said to me, "I wish I received feedback more often. I'd like to know how I'm doing, and how to improve." Another employee at the center said, "I wish we were held accountable for following the rules. Yeah, I break the rules, but no one's doing anything about it, so..."

Without a system for accountability in place and used regularly, the center's culture tends to gravitate to the lowest common denominator. The QA program offers this system, and when properly implemented, it acts as a safety net to prevent the entire center from dropping to its lowest possible levels.

<u>Self-Assessment</u>

1. How frequently are you taking time to sit down with your TCs to applaud them for the great work they do each day and to review areas of improvement?
2. Is your QA program used to build people up or tear people down?

CHAPTER 16
IF YOU DON'T COACH THEM, THEY WON'T LEARN

In addition to frequency of feedback, the other important aspect is how you share it. The most effective leaders are those who have mastered the art of using coaching for providing feedback. In their 2018 Harvard Business Review article, Julia Milner and Trenton Milner share their research showing how most in a leadership role don't know what it means to provide coaching. "For one thing, managers tend to think they're coaching when they're actually just telling their employees what to do."

According to Sir John Whitmore, a leading figure in executive coaching, the definition of coaching is "unlocking a person's potential to maximize their own performance. It is helping them to learn rather than teaching them." When done right, coaching can also help with employee engagement; it is often more motivating to bring your expertise to a situation than to be told what to do, especially when it comes to headstrong 9-1-1 professionals.

In the Milners' study, a group of participants was asked to coach another person on the topic of time management, without further explanation. The coaching conversations lasted five minutes and were videotaped. Later, other research participants evaluated the tapes, as did eighteen coaching experts. The experts each had a master's degree or graduate certificate in coaching, with an average of 23 years' work experience and 7 years' coaching experience.

The biggest takeaway was that, when initially asked to coach, many managers instead demonstrated a form of consulting. Essentially, they simply provided the other person with advice or a solution. They used comments like, "First you do this" or "Why don't you do this?" This kind of micromanaging-as-coaching was initially reinforced as good coaching practice by other research participants. The evaluations peers gave one another were significantly higher than the evaluations from experts. The research also found that managers can be trained to be better coaches if we start by defining what coaching actually looks like.

In 9-1-1, the strongest inclination is to tell someone what to do. "There's no time to beat around the bush! Officer safety is at risk!" This is true not only for the emergency situations that arise in the center, but also for conversations that have the *potential* to be coaching conversations. Instead of asking questions that might further the exploration of the reasons why something was done, supervisors tell an employee what they did wrong in a punitive tone and then send them on their way. This is another missed opportunity.

The distinction Whitmore makes—"helping someone to learn" vs "teaching them"—can be a tough one to make. If you're not sure how to make the switch from "telling" to "coaching," it can help to work with a model. The following model was originally developed in the 1980s by business coaches Graham Alexander, Alan Fine, and Sir John Whitmore.

THE GROW MODEL

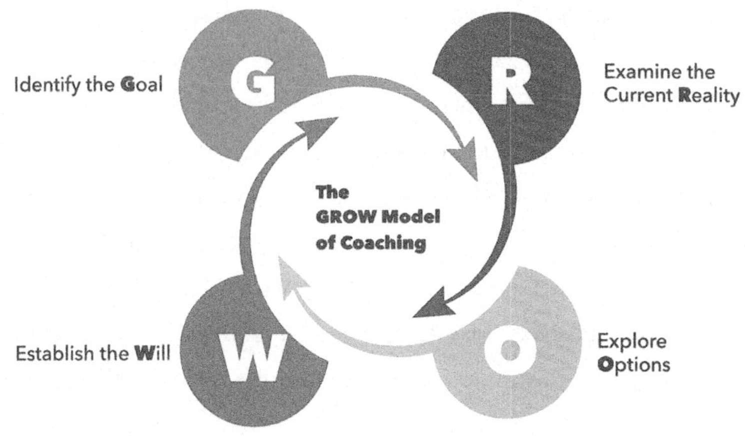

1. Identify the **G**oal

    First, you and your team member need to look at the behavior you want to change, and then structure this change as a goal that she wants to achieve.

    Make sure that this is a SMART goal: one that is specific, measurable, attainable, realistic, and time-bound.

    When doing this, it's useful to ask these questions:

    1. How will you know when your team member has achieved this goal?
    2. How will you know when the problem or issue is solved?
    3. Does this goal fit with her overall career objectives?
    4. Does it fit with the team's objectives?

2. Examine the Current **R**eality

    Next, ask your team member to describe his current reality.

    This is an important step. Too often, people try to solve a problem or reach a goal without fully considering their starting point, and often they're missing some information they need in order to reach their goal effectively. As your team member tells you about his current reality, the solution may start to emerge.

    Useful coaching questions in this step include the following:

    1. What is happening now (what, who, when, and how often)?
    2. What is the effect or result of this?
    3. Have you already taken any steps towards your goal?
    4. Does this goal conflict with any other goals or objectives?

3. Explore the **O**ptions

    Once you and your team member have explored the current reality, it's time to determine what is possible; this means you review all the potential options for reaching her objective.

    Help your team member brainstorm as many good options as possible. Then, discuss these and help her decide on the best ones.

By all means, offer your own suggestions in this step. But let your team member offer suggestions first and let her do most of the talking. It's important to *guide* her in the right direction without actually making decisions for her.

Typical questions you can use to explore options are as follows:

1. What else could you do?
2. What if this or that constraint was removed?
3. Would that change things?
4. What are the advantages and disadvantages of each option?
5. What factors or considerations will you use to weigh the options?
6. What do you need to stop doing in order to achieve this goal?
7. What obstacles stand in your way?

4. Establish the **Will**

By examining the current reality and exploring the options, your team member will now have a good idea of how he can achieve his goal.

While that's great, it may not be enough in itself. The final step is to get your team member to commit to specific actions in order to move towards his goal. Doing this will help him establish his will and boost his motivation.

Here are some useful questions to ask:

- So, what will you do now, and when?
- What else will you do?
- What could stop you from moving forward?
- How will you overcome this potential obstacle?
- How can you keep yourself motivated?
- How often do you need to review progress?

Finally, decide on a date when you'll both review his progress. This will provide some accountability and allow him to change his approach if the original plan isn't working.

This process continues with each conversation and each goal you and your team set out to achieve.

Switching from a telling to a coaching model of offering feedback has the power to turn the employee into a partner in their professional development instead of being relegated to the status of "punished." One supervisor at a comm center in Texas experienced this transition with his own employee.

The supervisor had been dreading a scheduled conversation with a problem employee at his center. He was anxious about having to discipline the employee and the reaction it might provoke. Before going into the conversation, the supervisor considered taking a different approach than in the past. Instead of telling the employee what the problem was, he decided to turn it into a coaching conversation.

He began by sharing his goal for the conversation. He articulated an objective that was focused on a positive outcome for the employee, which disarmed her. When we're gearing up for a fight, we tend to tense up for the coming onslaught. Because the employee didn't have to worry about what her supervisor was going to say next, she was able to relax some. The supervisor then asked the employee to describe her current reality.

Going into the exchange, the supervisor feared that much of what the employee was going through on the job had something to do with something he had said or guidance he hadn't provided (or that she would blame it on him). As she described her current reality, she confessed that much of the way she was showing up on the job—negative attitude, doing only the bare minimum, not following up properly—was because of a situation that she was dealing with at home. She admitted that she wasn't very good at keeping it from affecting her work, but she agreed that she could and should be doing more to prevent it from spilling out into the comm center.

Together, the employee and supervisor explored possible options forward. The work-related behavior was the focus of the conversation, but the context of what was going on with the employee at home mattered also. The employee agreed on two specific things she could be doing differently on the job and addressed the home situation as something that could derail the accomplishment of these goals. By the end of the meeting, the employee had decided on two specific outcomes that, if achieved, would be a success for the employee and for the center. The supervisor and employee agreed to meet again in two weeks to evaluate the employee's progress.

When the supervisor recounted this story, he remarked on two things. The first was the gratitude the employee expressed after feeling truly heard. The second was how much longer the conversation took than he expected. It's true that it takes more time to have this type of conversation than it does to have the old "listen to me while I tell you" conversation. It takes time to meet the other person where *they're* at and to relate to them on their terms. Leaders at the best centers know this, and they plan accordingly. The supervisor above had set aside the time for this conversation to happen in whatever timeframe it needed to. As a result, the employee re-engaged in her job. She emerged from the conversation with the feeling that her boss—and thereby, her organization—had her best interest in mind.

While it *cost* a bit more time, the *value* of an employee feeling this way about where she works is more than worth it.

Self-Assessment

1. How "tell-y" are you when you talk to other people? If you are perceived as a lecturer who is condescending, your words may not have their desired effect.
2. How often do you ask questions in order to know how to adjust your approach according to the person you're speaking with?
3. Are you a coach/mentor to your people? Do they feel like you have their backs?
4. What measures can you take to help your people feel more supported?

CHAPTER 17

THE POWER OF EMPLOYEE ENGAGEMENT

When dispensed in the proper way, regular feedback leads to enhanced employee engagement. Engaged employees have made an emotional commitment to the organization and its goals. They actually care about their work and the center they work for. They don't work just for a paycheck but on behalf of what the organization wants to achieve. When employees care—when they are engaged—they use discretionary effort on behalf of the organization. That means they show up and do a great job, not because they're being paid to, but because they believe in the impact they're making through their work at the center.

Employee engagement is different than employee happiness and employee satisfaction. These terms deal only with contentment, and don't address employees' level of motivation, involvement or true commitment.

We can categorize this level of emotional commitment in five ways. Employees at your center are either:

1. **Actively engaged**—Comprising 5-15% of the staff, these are the highest performers who can transform a mundane workplace into a hotbed of innovation, productivity, and fun. These employees feel such passion and connection with what they do and whom they do it with, they have more physiological resources to tackle large, daunting issues. These A players also motivate other, less engaged workers to increase their level of engagement for the period of time they work together.

2. **Engaged**—At the same time, another 20-25% of staff work at this level. They are focused on and deliver an honest day's work. Their outlook is positive, they work hard, and they generally believe in the mission and vision.
3. **Almost engaged**—This 5-10% has the potential to join the next level, if they could catch more than a glimpse of how their career vision lines up with the center's vision. They are willing to do more, but also willing to leave if something better comes along.
4. **Somewhat disengaged**—Roughly half the staff is here. They are clock-punchers who generally do adequate work but are not functioning anywhere near their full potential. For any number of reasons, they are distracted for 2-3 hours each day, disrupting the workflow and quality for coworkers who disdain their presence.
5. **Actively disengaged**—The final 5-15% of the workforce has checked out completely but still want the paycheck. These are people who actively doubt the center mission and vision, speak poorly of the organization and its leaders, and do just enough to not get called on the carpet or fired. These employees often act out and are the most resistant to change.

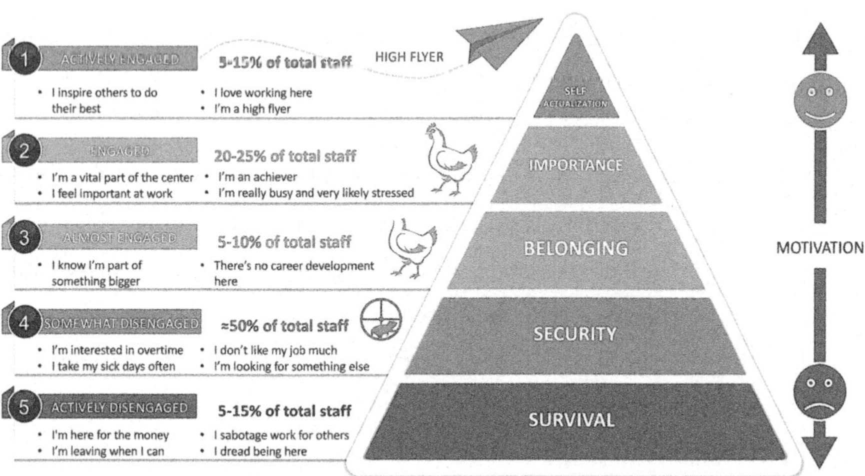

Gallup, the research and analytics company behind the "Gallup polls" you've likely heard of, has done a tremendous amount of research into the power of employee engagement, and the statistics are shocking:

- Teams with high employee engagement rates are 21% more productive and have 28% less internal theft than those with low engagement
- Disengaged workers had 37% higher absenteeism, 49% more accidents, and 60% more errors and defects
- Employees who are engaged are 27% more likely to report "excellent" performance
- Managers account for at least 70% of the variance in engagement scores

So, engagement matters for long-term success, and leadership matters for engagement. Performance management through feedback is one way to promote more engagement, and there are several more, including the following that are being actively used by the centers mentioned in this book:

1. Create structures and processes to link employees' roles and tasks to a larger mission and purpose.
2. Develop and maintain clear expectations about employees' tasks, roles, and decision-making authority.
3. Create transparently fair processes to reward employees and to encourage outstanding efforts.
4. Involve employees appropriately in diagnosing and solving problems, making decisions, and implementing ideas.
5. Create, authorize, and support small groups and teams to take on important, prominent assignments.
6. Invest prominently in selecting, training, evaluating, and rewarding highly competent supervisors and leaders.

The clarity of your center's mission and vision provides the context for the above actions to take place. A climate survey asked how employees in a small center in northwestern Unites States felt about their job. Nearly every employee reported feeling that the work they do is "very meaningful," yet morale was still lagging. Feeling your work is very meaningful goes a long way, but if you don't feel like your organization's mission and values are aligned with your own or that your efforts are making a difference, the meaningfulness of your work may not translate into engagement on the job.

An organization's leadership absolutely impacts employee engagement. Employees who know why they're working so hard, and what they're working for, come together more readily during tough times. More importantly, they are a functioning team when it's business as usual.

Self-Assessment

1. How committed are the majority of your people, from the perspective of the five levels of employee engagement? If you have no way to objectively measure your center's engagement level, administering an anonymous survey is a great way to go. If you fear that you won't get real feedback because the state of your center's culture, contracting a third party to help collect this information is effective.
2. What's something you can do to improve employee engagement? If you're not sure, this is a great question to pose to your team.

APPRECIATION, RECOGNITION & MOTIVATION

As discussed throughout the book, the best centers in this country have several things in common. The most pronounced is the way and the frequency with which center leaders show their appreciation for whom they work with. These leaders say things like, "I work for *them;* they don't work for me." "My job is to make their job easier." "I look out for my people, because I can't do this myself. They are our greatest asset." "My job is about spending quality time with my employees and going the extra mile."

In James Hunter's seminal leadership classic *The Servant: A Simple Story About the True Essence of Leadership*, he speaks to where this sentiment comes from:

Love.

Hunter further qualifies this pronouncement by saying, "It's not how you feel, but how you behave. It's built upon influence, which is built upon service and sacrifice, which is built upon love." The leadership values of patience, kindness, empathy, humility, respectfulness, selflessness, forgiveness, honesty, commitment all flow from this.

Lynn Bowler, former Support Services Manager for Elk Grove Police Department in California and a 37-year veteran of the 9-1-1 industry, when asked how she successfully inspires trust and positive change replied, "I have a genuine love and concern for people who do this job, and I'm committed to making things better for them, always."

LaDonna Coriell, former Marshall County E911 Director, says, "Caring about people is my #1 opportunity. My employees love me, and say it, and I love them."

Virgin CEO Richard Branson puts it succinctly when he says, "Clients do not come first. Employees come first. If you take care of your employees, they will take care of the clients."

This level of commitment from a leader inspires commitment, but it can't be faked. It has to be real and demonstrated daily. When it is, amazing things happen.

One assistant director at a center in the southern US was holding his breath for a better situation when the old director at his center was fired and a new one was hired. The incoming director understood leadership and was invested in improving things. Within months, the new director's efforts began to bear fruit. The culture shifted, working conditions improved, and employees re-engaged with the job they loved. Recently, when asked about the changes he's seen happen, the assistant director said, "I used to hate coming into work. I truly thought getting this job was the worst mistake I'd ever made. Now, I've never been prouder of the place I work."

They say in the military, "The shit rolls downhill." But so does the good stuff. Fostering a climate of appreciation, and thereby motivation, begins with appreciating the person sitting next to you, or saying "Hi" when you walk by someone in the cramped hallway of the comm center. It's no more or less simple than getting into an attitude of gratitude. As Irwin Federman, known for his corporate turnaround efforts while leading troubled semiconductor manufacturer Monolithic Memories, once put it, "This business of making another person feel good in the unspectacular course of his/her daily comings and goings is, in my view, the very essence of leadership."

At one large center in western US, the director told his supervisors, "If you're going to have an exchange with an employee that the employee might perceive as negative [constructive feedback, discipline, remediation, etc.], you must first have had three positive exchanges with this employee. And you must maintain this three positive to one-negative ratio at all times." According to a study that examined the effectiveness of leadership teams found that *ideal* positive-to-negative ratio is closer to six to one, but you have to start somewhere!

Think of the shift that a three-positive to one-negative ratio would have on your center. If it's true that "the only time we ever hear anything is when it's bad," then making a concerted effort to say something positive goes a long way towards changing this age-old comm center norm.

I shared the above story with a room of supervisors at a recent conference, and someone in the front row said, "That just seems inauthentic. You mean, if I call someone into my office, I have to say, 'Your uniform looks nice today. Thanks for being here and not calling in sick. Your coworkers seem to like you. Ok, now here's the real reason I called you in here: sign this complaint review form.'"

It's clear that this supervisor missed the point. To maintain this ratio and not be seen as a manipulator, it may take some effort to find opportunities to acknowledge your people. And there are many. How many exchanges does each employee have with the public in the course of one day? How many overtime shifts are picked up, shifts traded, jobs done well? These are *all* opportunities to walk by a console and say, "Thanks for doing that."

Some supervisors say, "It's not my job to improve someone's morale. Their attitude is their problem." On one level, it's true that you can't make someone want to be somewhere they don't want to be. You can't offer them an "attitude adjustment," as my dad used to say. However, the best leaders first ask themselves, "Am I doing everything within *my* power to make this an environment where positivity and motivation can thrive?"

It takes work to make daily recognition a habit, but it's the daily habit that's going to improve things the most. Some agencies pride themselves on how big a celebration they're able to put together for Telecommunicator's Week. This is fantastic, and necessary, but if once a year is the only time the team hears they are doing a great job and someone is noticing, it's not enough. What if someone is on vacation or days off during this time? Then they *never* hear that their efforts are noticed?

An organization's culture flows from the daily interactions that most people take for granted. Said in another way, it's the small stuff that matters most.

One center fosters a climate of appreciation and inclusion with a "brag board." Team members get to share important personal news, anniversaries, and accomplishments with each other. Another center features one employee each month, whose answers to three interesting questions about themselves are posted on the board. Another center identifies the outstanding calls through their QA process and puts the names of those who took the calls in a drawing. At the end of the month, a name is drawn, and that person gets to select a prize. Yet another center has a bulletin board with a silly picture of every employee on it, with a fun fact about that person next to their picture. Fellow employees are encouraged to post notes of appreciation next to their photo. The board is overflowing with notes!

Employees recognizing each other is important, but it can't overpower the effects of absentee or negative leadership. If the team comes together to create a positive environment, yet the director, manager or supervisors don't participate, it doesn't mean that leadership doesn't matter. It means the team came together *despite* weak leadership. The initiatives outlined in this book are much easier to achieve when leadership is on board and guiding the process.

Many who've been in the industry a long time say, "It's a kinder, friendlier comm center we're building. Isn't that special?" in a dryly sarcastic manner. Sometimes it's chalked up to generational differences. "Oh, these snowflakes," the tenured folks lament, "they just don't know how to work hard. They want it all but aren't willing to put in the time."

The problem with this line of thinking is that it misses something huge. The modern organization has evolved in the past 30 years. A lot. Private businesses have always had a strong incentive to evolve as quickly as possible: shareholder value, profits, revenue. Without a similar intent driving the industry into more worthwhile frontiers, 9-1-1 is quite frankly behind the times—about 30 years behind, actually. But there are ways to get it back on track.

HERZBERG'S TWO-FACTOR THEORY

In 1959, behavioral scientist Frederick Herzberg proposed a two-factor theory or the motivator-hygiene theory. According to Herzberg, some job factors result in satisfaction while other job factors prevent dissatisfaction.

What Herzberg called "hygiene factors" are elements of one's job that are essential for the existence of motivation at the workplace and extrinsic to the work itself. These factors do not lead to long-term satisfaction, but their absence leads to *dis*satisfaction. In other words, hygiene factors are those which, when adequate/reasonable in a job, pacify the employees and do not make them dissatisfied. These are also called maintenance factors, as they are required to avoid dissatisfaction. They represent the physiological needs that people want and expect to be fulfilled.

Hygiene factors include the following:

- **Pay**—An appropriate and reasonable pay structure that is equal and competitive to those in the same industry in the same area.
- **Company policies**—The company policies should not be too rigid, and be fair and clear. They should include flexibility with shift rotations, dress code, breaks, vacation, etc.
- **Fringe benefits**—Employees should be offered healthcare plans, benefits for the family members, employee assistance programs, etc.
- **Physical working conditions**—Working conditions should be safe, clean and hygienic, and equipment should be updated and well-maintained.
- **Status**—The employees' status within the organization should be familiar and retained.
- **Interpersonal relations**—The relationship of each employee with their peers, superiors and subordinates should be appropriate and acceptable. There should be no conflict or condescension present.
- **Job security**—The organization must provide job security to the employees.

According to Herzberg, hygiene factors above are not motivators; they merely *prevent dissatisfaction*. The motivational factors, on the other hand, yield positive satisfaction. They are inherent to the work itself and motivate employees towards superior performance. Employees find these intrinsically rewarding, and they represent the psychological needs that are perceived as an additional benefit.

Motivational factors include the following:

- **Recognition**—Employees should receive praise and recognition from their managers for their accomplishments.
- **Sense of achievement**—Employees must have a sense of achievement in the course of their daily work duties.
- **Growth and promotional opportunities**—There must be growth and advancement opportunities in an organization to motivate the employees to perform well.
- **Responsibility**—Employees hold themselves responsible for the work. Managers give them ownership, minimize control and promote accountability.
- **Meaningfulness of the work**—The work itself should be meaningful, interesting and challenging.

How do we interpret Herzberg's theory and its application to 9-1-1? From the outset, the most important point is that eliminating the causes of dissatisfaction (hygiene factors) will not create satisfaction. It will merely create a situation whereby the person is neither satisfied nor dissatisfied. For example, let's say a comm center pays less than similar centers in the area, and substandard policies create a negative and hostile work environment. Simply giving employees a raise and writing new policies will not suddenly create motivated workers.

This seems counterintuitive and is likely the cause for why so many comm center administrators say things like, "No matter what we do, the employees just don't seem happy. We raised their pay, built a new center with new equipment, *and* hired in a new director!" However, Herzberg found that when these elements—pay, working conditions, interpersonal relations—are at an acceptable level, they allow the employee to go from "dissatisfied" to "neutral," and no further. A motivating environment, one where people like to work, must have a combination of both hygiene factors *and* motivating factors.

When *both* factors are present, change can happen quickly. When pay is brought up to market level, a new manager is hired who is better with the people than the previous manager, *AND* employees get recognized with new promotional opportunities, it both removes hygiene factors creating dissatisfaction and introduces motivating factors. This is what it means to create a motivating environment for our people.

The research is conclusive: people would rather come into a job that makes them feel appreciated. Sure, hardened veterans of emergency services—veterans of the "suck-it-up" culture—might construe that people want to work less and receive more. But really, people want to be happy, and if their job is preventing them from being happy, they'll quit. Now, more than any other time in human history, we have the ability to ask for what we want and then go about finding it. Blame it on the internet, blame it on social media, blame it on whatever you'd like. It's a *good* thing.

It's also a good thing when, given so many other options, someone chooses to work for your comm center. Each day, people are choosing to go into work, or not. Are we creating a workplace that makes this an easy choice? In which direction?

Self-Assessment

1. Are you helping to create a motivating or de-motivating work environment for your people?
2. What can you do every day to acknowledge your people for the work they do?

CHAPTER 18

TRAINING AND DEVELOPMENT

Providing regular feedback, coaching your people, and showing appreciation for their efforts on a regular basis can all drive higher levels of engagement. Yet nothing drives a larger wedge between employee and supervisor than employees feeling they lack the tools to succeed in their jobs. Without frequent, ongoing training opportunities, we shouldn't be surprised when our prized employees wither on the vine and leave for another opportunity that provides a better chance for personal growth.

I've found that the best centers consistently spend much more time and money on training than the rest. They prioritize the allocation of these funds and then spend the dollars every year. You might think, "I'd spend more on training if they would give me more money," or "We'll do something about training when our staffing is better." The problem with waiting and not doing anything is that nothing will change, and things will likely get worse. The stories I've been told point to a similar thread: initiative matters. Every leader I spoke to took action immediately, wherever and however they could. From a few thousand to millions of dollars, agencies that previously had "no money" for improvements were able to find funding much more quickly than imagined; in some cases, the funds were made available simply because someone had the courage to ask.

One new director, who was in her position for just a few months at the time, addressed the county fiscal court on behalf of her center and requested money for a new facility and new consoles. She was told time after time, "It can't be done. Sorry." But she kept going to bat for her people. In the meantime, she found some money for training. "There was a 'miscellaneous' line item on my budget—it wasn't much, but it helped—and I sent a few of my people to a local training class," she said. Her team was nominated for an award at the state 9-1-1 conference, and she went to the county treasurer and insisted, "We're going to this conference. I don't care where the money comes from or if I have to pay for it myself. We're all going." The county found the money, and the entire team attended the conference (for their first time). She kept harassing the "powers that be" for more money to improve working conditions for her people. Recently, her tenacity paid off. Her center is breaking ground for a new communications facility in a month, with new consoles and a new radio system. One employee said, "We've never had someone speak up on our behalf for something we need."

Training is essential, both for new hires *and* for those already working. It gives new hires the skills that breed confidence while working the console. Research shows that trainees who don't feel prepared feel more stress as a result of the job, whereas those who feel like they have the tools to succeed are more likely rise to the occasion and less likely to become traumatized early in their career. A hallmark of more resilient people is their belief that they will overcome the challenges they meet. Managers can help their trainees foster this belief and the attendant self-confidence by giving them the training necessary to succeed.

I was surprised when traveling around the country to learn how few agencies observe a minimum training standard for their TCs. In fact, only 27 states have state-mandated training guidelines and offer the state funding required to enforce these guidelines. Some comm centers do two weeks of classroom training, a couple weeks of observation with a CTO, and then new employees are working a console solo. Some centers do two weeks of training, period. That's it. These centers are also more likely to pay a much smaller starting wage, seemingly reflective of the value the area and the agency places on retaining TCs.

For tenured employees, training is the career development they need to stay engaged. Several studies show that most leave the profession at around the 7-year mark (they don't call it the "7-year itch" for nothing). It's my theory that at this point, you've done the job so long you can do it in your sleep. There's no more challenge to it, and the internal struggles of working in your center have become so frustrating that it seems impossible to justify putting in more hours.

Going to a training class at this point in one's career can offer a glimpse of a gap between where you are (skill-wise) and where you'd like to be. This awareness may help a TC who's "checked out" to re-engage and push pass this plateau. Training helps prevent the feeling of stagnation that's so common at this juncture.

The other importance of training your people is the application towards succession planning. Having a plan for who's going to step into the role above them will assure that the hard work you're doing to change the current culture continues for years to come. One exemplary leader said to me, "Every day, I'm training my replacement. If I'm not taking this particular role seriously, I shouldn't be surprised when there's no acceptable promotional candidates. If we don't have great people coming up through the ranks, we're in trouble."

It's clear that training matters for succession planning from the larger organizational perspective, and from the individual perspective as well. A perfectionist is much less willing to step into a new role if they don't feel prepared to do so. Providing training opportunities for employees to find out what they're good at, where they're interests lie, and how they can actualize this potential is vital for the center's future.

In nearly every study that addresses the challenges the 9-1-1 industry is facing, the author's concluding remarks recommend more and better leadership training opportunities at the comm center. As we've been exploring throughout this book, changing the state of industry is going to take intrepid leadership on a massive scale. Many in leadership roles at comm centers across the country don't even possess a cohesive understanding of what leadership *means*. While this is one of the biggest challenges, it's also a tremendous opportunity.

At the present time, a job in 9-1-1 is entry level. It requires just a high school diploma, and much, if not all, of the training and education a 9-1-1 professional receives comes from their employing agency. This is a responsibility that mustn't be taken lightly. If the only qualification a prospective supervisory candidate brings to the table is "20 years on the job," we're in trouble. The context for what constitutes "leadership success" must be taught, and that ability honed through practice. The best front line dispatcher may not turn out to be the best supervisor or leader.

Being a great leader encompasses many things, a great deal of which we've covered throughout this book: interpersonal skills, coaching ability, communication and conflict resolution skills, emotional intelligence, to name a few. Training can and will absolutely improve these abilities, and it can happen more quickly than one might think. Remember the study cited in Chapter 16 that found most managers don't know how to have coaching conversations? The second part of that study included giving the managers face-to-face training on how to be a better coach. After this short session, the managers were found to have improved over 40% across nine different coaching skills.

Training matters. When it's missing, the people in our centers stop growing. As Lou Holtz once said, "You're either growing or you're dying." This is doubly true for the type A overachievers who work the console. We have to give them both something to grow into and the means to do so.

THE IMPORTANCE OF CONFERENCES

The state and national conferences for the national 9-1-1 trade associations also offer employees an excellent opportunity to learn from others in their profession, understand their role in the larger 9-1-1 family, and get the training they need. Some centers reward exceptional performance by an employee with an opportunity to attend a conference. When such a reward is contextualized and connected to the center's larger mission and values, it raises the reward's value in the employees' eyes.

I was a front line telecommunicator for over 10 years and didn't know I was part of a global community of those who worked in the profession. It wasn't until after I started offering training classes at conferences that I learned this. Stepping outside of your organization's silo can shed light on old issues that other centers have solved. It can help you to know you're not alone, and it can offer a pathway to something different.

ADVANCEMENT OPPORTUNITY

Aside from regular training, the other aspect of career development is having somewhere to go. The centers where people like coming to work offer opportunities for their employees to apply themselves in a way that's authentic to them. This is really about creating ownership. When you give someone something to own, it's theirs.

Ivan Whitaker found at Polk County that it mattered a great deal to give team members a voice and the ability to give input into something that was going to affect their work lives. As Ivan also discovered, you don't have to promote everyone into higher-paying roles or create new spots in the hierarchy. Advancement opportunities can include seats on any of a variety of committees, a tactical dispatch role, "expert" status on console technology, or union steward. Any role that will help advance the center as a whole is an advancement opportunity for the person appointed, if communicated accordingly.

Self-Assessment

1. What is your center's current succession planning strategy?
2. How do you prepare your employees for advancement opportunities?
3. What additional opportunities are needed to keep your best people, and what measures can you take to create them?

CHAPTER 19

PRIORITIZE EMPLOYEE HEALTH

In 2007, a study was published—the first of its kind—exploring the connection between duty-related trauma in 9-1-1 and PSTD symptoms. 9-1-1 professionals had known all along that the job took a toll, but this was the first conclusive glimpse into the toll this career could take. Since that pioneering research, many more studies have followed, some with similar conclusions. Still others have deepened our understanding of what takes place at the mental, emotional and physical levels when someone works for years in this profession.

The studies point to vicarious trauma, secondary traumatic stress, compassion fatigue, and emotional labor. They show that the rate of morbid obesity, meaning an individual is 100 lbs. or more over their ideal body weight, is 50% higher in our comm centers than the general population. They reflect the reality that working in a job while dealing with the stress and trauma of others can create stress of its own. On a positive note, the studies also point to opportunities for lessening the job's impact. They show that those who work in the profession can take preventative measures to thrive in a role that allows one to make a difference in a personal and powerful way.

Your employees' mental and physical health are just one dimension of a people-oriented approach, and often one that we leave to the individual. But study after study concludes that organizations who take their employees' health into consideration enjoy higher degrees of employee engagement, lower healthcare spending, and higher morale. One study featured in the *Journal of Occupational Environmental Medicine* found that healthy employees took 40% less sick days each. Another study found that on average, for every $1 employers spend on worker medical or pharmacy costs, they absorb at least $2 to $4 of health-related productivity costs in the form of absenteeism and presenteeism associated with chronic conditions.

Aside from providing healthcare benefits that include access to wellness resources and mental health professionals, there are proactive measures that comm centers can take every day to positively impact employee health. The APCO Project RETAINS Effective Practices Guide highlighted the operational decisions that impact staffing and retention, many of which reflect creating a healthier workplace.

The five primary factors that contribute to retention that we discussed in Chapter 1, as contained in Project RETAINS, are all related to employee health:

1. Fully staffed (all authorized positions filled)
2. Monthly overtime hours
3. Job complexity
4. Hourly base pay
5. Working conditions

Each of these factors impacts an employee's ability to show up day after day to work an already taxing job. Multi-tasking, a necessary skill when it comes to working a 9-1-1 console, takes willpower to sustain. It also takes making the choice to say the right words to coworkers and callers. Willpower is a finite resource. You have the most at the start of your day; as you make decisions, that supply dwindles.

Researcher Kathleen Vohs, professor of marketing at the Carlson School of Management at University of Minnesota, put it this way in a *Prevention* magazine article in 2009: "Willpower is like gas in your car… When you resist something tempting, you use some up. The more you resist, the emptier your tank gets, until you run out of gas." It becomes more difficult over time to make accurate decisions and to stay sharp as we switch from task to task, making fast-paced decisions with citizen and officer safety at risk. When your store of willpower is gone, you are more likely to fall back to your default settings—like negative thinking or eating junk food.

There hasn't been a formal study of the impact of short staffing, overtime, and 9-1-1 professionals doing more work with less people. However, a study conducted in Israel explored the impact of willpower on the Israeli parole system, and we can use this to draw some of the same conclusions about comm centers.

The researchers analyzed 1,112 parole board hearings assigned to eight judges over a ten-month period (which amounted to 40% of Israel's total parole requests over that period). The pace is grueling. The judges hear arguments and take about six minutes to render a decision on 14 to 35 parole requests a day, and they get only two breaks—a morning snack and a late lunch—to rest and refuel. The impact of their schedule is as spectacular as it is surprising: in the mornings and after each break, parolees' chances for being released peak at 65%, and then plunge to near zero by the end of each period (see figure below).

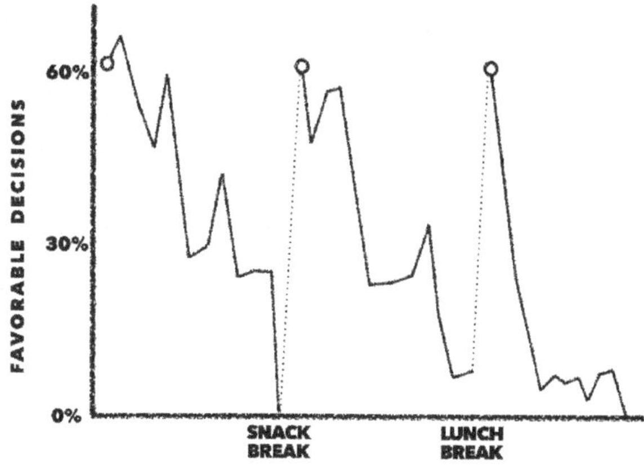

The results are most likely tied to the mental toll of repetitive decision making. These are big decisions for the parolees and the public at large. High stakes and the assembly-line rhythm demand intense focus throughout the day. As their energy is spent, judges mentally collapse into their "default choice,"

which doesn't turn out so well for the hopeful prisoners—since the default decision for a parole judge is no. When in doubt and willpower is low, the prisoner stays behind bars.

This is not unlike the average day someone in the comm center experiences: processing call after call, broadcast after broadcast, interaction after interaction. At the end of a shift, how likely is a 9-1-1 professional to make the healthy food choice or lace-up the athletic shoes and go get some exercise? Making a positive shift, when everyone else around you is a Negative Nelly or a Pissy Pete, also requires willpower.

The study above points to the power of willpower, along with the importance of taking breaks and eating the right kind of food. The brain consumes 20% of the body's resources (oxygen from breathing and glucose from food) while accounting for only a small fraction of the body's total mass. With no time to eat and no time take a break (I'm amazed at how many centers don't allow their TCs any breaks), it's no wonder it becomes so difficult to change one's behavior, even when we know it's the right thing to do. Met with these challenges, many leave the profession, not because they "can't hack it," but because they've grown wise to the importance of prioritizing their own health.

If the nature of the job is to multi-task and make life-or-death decisions every day, then creating an environment where someone performing these duties can thrive is critical to the correct functioning of the entire 9-1-1 system. You can have all the best technology, but if you don't have people to do the work, it's not worth anything.

The Project RETAINS study results were released in 2005. We've known about the five primary factors affecting center retention for at least this amount of time. Yet centers are still understaffed, employees are still getting crushed by OT (both voluntary and mandatory), pay is shockingly low in some areas of the country, and the working conditions are atrocious—paint chipping off the walls of the center, old chairs and consoles, and computer systems from 1995 causing a new generation of workers to learn DOS-based command prompts when there are much more efficient ways of operating.

Some will say, "Well, it still works." That isn't a valid argument. A horse-drawn carriage still works, but cars are much more efficient. Cassette tapes still work but streaming via Bluetooth is more efficient.

In what areas of your comm center are you applying reactive thought processes to justify not taking action? Where are you waiting for someone to die before you're forced to take decisive action? It might sound harsh, but it's so often the case in our industry that changes aren't made until a tragic call results in death. Denise Amber Lee. Sebastian Caban. Kyle Plush. In the aftermath of each one of these deadly incidents, sweeping changes were made at the local, state and national levels, resulting in the release of millions of dollars of support that weren't available prior to the event. But it's a shame it had to come to this. Risk management expert, author, and speaker Gordon Graham always says these are "problems lying in wait," and "predictable is preventable."

It's easy to blame the lack of money for less-than-full staffing and the resulting effects, but I think it's more a specific mindset we must overcome as an industry. We tend to think there isn't value in prioritizing the health of those who work in the communications center, or we haven't clearly defined the benefit of creating an environment that's conducive to good health. On the contrary, the communications center has been a characteristically *unhealthy* environment—from windowless rooms with low ceilings and stained floors to office chairs not rated for 24-hour use and consoles having nothing to do with ergonomics.

This is changing, with amazing equipment providers like Watson, Evans, Russ Bassett, Concept Seating, and others offering solutions that twenty years ago didn't even exist. What is the leading frontier, then, when it comes prioritizing employee health at the comm center?

BRING EXPECTATIONS IN LINE WITH REALITY

There are things that must be done first with regard to the five factors impacting retention. Living up to the expectations set forth by the larger organization the center is a part of it; adjusting outdated organizational expectations to bring them more in line with today's reality is next.

During a recent consulting project, I was asked to assist a center that had grappled with low morale and high trainee turnover for several years, with employee sentiment on a gradual decline during that time. Center executive management wanted me to help them get a better understanding of the underlying issues and to make recommendations for improvement. During the assessment phase of the project, we learned that the center manager didn't feel that the number of authorized positions was accurate. He asserted that the center didn't need any more dispatchers on shift during any given watch. He claimed that while the team was working overtime every week, the salary spending for the communications division was several hundred thousand dollars under budget. The manager felt these cost savings were more than justification for keeping the staffing numbers as they were, despite the fact that the challenges faced by this center—low morale, retention issues, trainee washout—were directly related to frequent OT.

Because the manager didn't see value in getting the center to full staff, he didn't prioritize hiring. He wasn't an advocate for making the recruitment, hiring and training process more effective, and he didn't help the supervisory staff with their duties when they were required to work the floor (which was the norm). The manager's perspective is understandable, but it reveals a lack of understanding about the true impact of frequent OT. The manager didn't know that because of years of working at minimum staffing with OT...

- Supervisors were burning out because, in addition to the tasks they were promoted to manage, they also worked the dispatch floor more frequently.
- Burned-out supervisors were more likely to take the frustrations with both management and their center situation out on their team members.

- The center operated on a "voluntold" OT selection process. In other words, while OT shifts were not made mandatory, if an employee hadn't picked up an OT shift in the last rotation, they were strongly encouraged via group email to pick up a shift. This seeded discontentment and fostered in-fighting.
- Because supervisors were working the floor regularly, there was no time for proactive supervision, including call monitoring, EMD, weekly check-ins, or communication.
- Employees felt stagnant and like no one cared about their work and their professional development because there were no training or advancement opportunities.

This was clearly a center where staffing didn't permit proactive supervision, coaching conversations or regular feedback. In an environment such as this, the only thing employees have to look forward to is "more of the same" for years. The culture is assured to be bad, or it's currently suffering the downward spiral.

Another unhealthy situation comm center employees regularly face is that staffing levels don't correctly take into consideration the workload of the center. At a different center, their budgeted positions were fully staffed, yet employees were regularly required to work OT. This situation works for employees who don't mind working OT, but to require OT every week because the staffing figures aren't accurate sends a message to employees that they're expendable.

THE EXPENDABLES

Prioritizing employee health by using staffing models that account for the fact that 9-1-1 employees want and need time off is a start. But where else is the industry sending employees the message that they are expendable?

Each of these five areas, repeated from the APCO RETAINS Effective Practices Guide, offer an opportunity to change things by helping your employees feel more valued:

1. Staffing situation (whether the center is fully staffed)
2. Average overtime hours per month
3. Job complexity
4. Hourly base pay rate
5. Employee satisfaction with working conditions

If your center is not fully staffed, and you're not actively working to get there—by every means possible—you're implicitly telling your employees they don't matter. While some employees might view high number of monthly OT hours as a benefit, this will cause even the most dedicated employee to leave. It isn't a vision of success when someone says that they've worked hundreds of hours of OT in the past year at the expense of every other area of their life. We can't require our employees to simply live to work. It's not sustainable. There's a reason why APCO coined overtime "the perverse incentive."

I'm certain there isn't a single public safety agency mission statement that reflects a desire to use up their employees to the point of them being forced out of a job they love. Yet this is the unfortunate career-ending decision many dedicated 9-1-1 professionals make.

In the book *What Happy Companies Know*, the authors make the case for a values-driven look at how an organization does *everything*—including hiring, staffing, pay, and working conditions. "For the happiest organizations," the authors write, "the presence of a meaningful mission, leadership integrity, and the proper consideration of their employees, their many other stakeholders, their customers, and their communities" is the combination that matters most to success. "A thoughtful balance is key."

When it comes to prioritizing its people, the 9-1-1 industry is anything but balanced. The vast majority of communications centers continue to grapple with the same issues, year-after-year, because someone in the hierarchy hasn't prioritized the right thing. The best centers know what this one thing is: the people under the headset.

Self-Assessment

1. Does your center's current staffing model reflect the reality that employees require breaks, and don't appreciate mandatory overtime?
2. Are your employees invited to participate in incident after-action debriefings, along with field responders?
3. Are you giving your employees the resources to thrive in a role that demands a great deal from them—mentally, physically and emotionally?
4. What more can be done at your center, from an employee health perspective, to care for your people?

PRIORITIZING YOUR PEOPLE IS ABOUT RISK AND LIABILITY

9-1-1 is unlike other "businesses" in a critical way: without enough high-quality, dedicated employees to work in the 9-1-1 center, our communities are at risk. And the citizens who count on a fully functioning 9-1-1 system when they need it are discovering that it isn't a fully functioning as they expect. This, in many ways, is cause for outrage. The community suffers when one of their constituents dies, but so does the 9-1-1 professional at the other end of the line, along with every other member of the center's team.

Again, predictable is preventable. We shouldn't be surprised when someone who's worked a 15-hour shift without a break 5 days in a row makes a mistake resulting in an injury or death. It's not surprising that opportunities for team synergy are being squandered or completely lost because management is stretched too thin to do anything but work the floor, just like everyone else. It makes sense that important details fall through the cracks when those in leadership roles are excusing bad behavior as "normal." It takes courage to look at "the way we've always done it," and say, "This is not acceptable."

It's not acceptable that most comm centers are miserable places to work. It's not acceptable that many 9-1-1 professionals *need* to work OT to make a wage that will provide for their families. It's not acceptable that, despite what we know about successful organizations and how they care for their employees, 9-1-1 still overlooks so many of these proven principles. It's not acceptable that more isn't being done—now, today—to curtail the exodus of qualified and dedicated professionals from a profession as rewarding as this.

But we have to change the perspective on how rewards are doled out in this profession. Yes, the work is meaningful, but even the most meaningful work causes motivation to eventually wane if those performing it don't receive a nominal wage. Without advancement opportunities available to more than just a few, stagnation is the norm. We can't count on always having more people to hire. Already, that is a doomed staffing philosophy. What happens when there's no one else left to force to work OT?

This is the importance of prioritizing people, for today and the long-term. Comm centers who are seen as advocates for their employees generate a very different feeling from those who adopt a "warm body is better than no body" staffing philosophy.

To stem the turnover, create a center where people like to work, and protect the communities and field responders we have sworn to protect, we must do better. It's a people driven approach, from within and without.

LOW STAFFING PREVENTS PROACTIVE MEASURES

One center in the western US had fallen on difficult times. After years of minimum staffing, low trainee success rates and little guidance from upper management, the supervisors decided to stop doing proactive QA. Their policy manual stated that, at a minimum, employees would be provided two call monitorings each month per EMD protocol. In the two years since disbanding the QA program, the center had hired several employees, all of whom had not been monitored proactively since their completion of the training program.

There are many implications of such a decision. From a risk and liability perspective, the EMD protocol exists to insure a standard level of patient pre-arrival care. If a center is unable or unwilling to uphold a standard for such an important element of center operations, we have to wonder: where else is the organization making concessions? From an accountability standpoint, employees who receive little or no feedback because the avenue for such feedback conversations no longer exists are left to run on the hamster wheel. They never know if their efforts are being noticed, if they matter or if they're good enough.

"No news is good news, I guess," employees are left thinking. But from a culture standpoint, a lack of integrity *never* goes unnoticed. Employees are always looking up the organizational hierarchy for an example to model. When a policy is disregarded due to factors that are seemingly within management's purview, employees interpret this as permission to fudge other policies. It's exceedingly difficult to hold staff accountable for violating expectations when you are violating expectations yourself.

Rather than let proactive QA fall by the wayside due to staffing, it's better to let other less important projects sit on the back burner. While the QA program was abandoned at the center cited above, supervisors received a laundry list of projects unrelated to daily center operations, furthering the perception by floor personnel that their professional growth was not important. These ancillary tasks included budgeting, going to meetings for which the manager was responsible, and pricing new equipment—tasks better handled by the manager.

Self-Assessment

1. What national standards does your center currently adhere to (APCO, NFPA, Priority Dispatch, etc.)?
2. Is your city/community/department/agency currently exposed to unnecessary risk and liability because of your center's staffing situation?

CHAPTER 20

DARE TO TELL A NEW STORY

Throughout the change management process, your center is invited to tell a new story—not a story of inherent deficiency, but of inherent greatness. Stories of greatness, of personal bests seen on the job and the positive impact we make on our communities, unlock energy not otherwise available. These stories provide the vision, and when imagined from the current reality, the excitement to do and be more.

Once you've made strides in the direction of positive change, it's the stories that will live on. If the story of your comm center is that it's a great place to work—one that inspires and enlivens you, and allows you to make the impact you're put here to make—it will inform how you show up, both on and off the job. There's a reason why all long-lasting companies have stories that they tell to remind them of where they came from, why they've persevered, and why they do what they do.

Melanie Neal, Director at Guilford Metro 9-1-1 in Greensboro, NC, worked for years to bring her center's current story to life. Three years after the consolidation that brought Guilford County and the City of Guilford under one roof, the situation hadn't improved. The biggest problem was that city personnel wasn't known for being friendly, and the county was. This disparity created animosity and team division. Further, the Ops Manager at the time had a habit of playing favorites and protecting those she liked.

As supervisor over a 23-person squad during this time, Melanie was aware of the optics of the favoritism. She knew it seeded discontentment. She saw the effects. When a line-level employee reported the bad behavior of one of the favorites, Melanie told the employee, "I agree something must be done, and I will follow up with you."

Melanie brought the concerns up to her boss, the Ops Manager, who said, "We're not going to do any paperwork." Melanie said, in response, "I assured [my employee] I would follow up, so you'll have to do something. *You* tell her why nothing has been done." Soon after, the Ops Manager was moved out of her position and Melanie was appointed to the position to make the necessary changes.

Within the first month, Melanie sat down with all four squads and communicated the expectations. The team was very supportive, for the most part. Out of 86 total employees, 75 were ready to make a change. The 10 or 11 who weren't on board made snide comments, saying, "We're not doing anything different. We've always done it this way."

The shake-up took about 14 months. With the new standard in place, Melanie and her team began holding people accountable for their actions. The discipline process wasn't swift, but it was necessary to go through each step. A 16-year employee and a 7-year employee were eventually let go because they refused to adhere to the new expectations. After a verbal warning, then a written warning, and then suspension (again, not quick, but necessary), they were finally dismissed.

Discipline was used only as a last resort. One of the biggest positive influencers of the change initiative was that Melanie set aside four hours each month to work in the room, which was something the previous manager never did. Initially, the team was concerned, and wondered, "Why is she here? Did we do something wrong?" Then they loved it. They saw she could do the job, and she was keeping her skills fresh. They realized that they could relate to her—that she was *one of them*.

Communicating expectations, setting a standard, and holding people accountable for maintaining this standard helped the center overcome its biggest challenge: bridging the gap between city and county employees. Five years after the consolidation, they realized the vision of "Guilford Metro"—instead of Guilford City and Guilford County—and became one.

Melanie took over after year three, and it took her two years of trying before her vision was realized. Even with 90% of staff supporting the effort and a compelling vision, it still took two years. For the first time, the county felt hopeful that customer service is where it needs to be for the people the center serves.

I asked Melanie what advice she has for the line-level supervisors who have lost hope. Despite the good they know they can do, these individuals often feel stuck between the employees they work for and the managers they work under. She shared the principles that have guided her during her 30+ year career:

> "Stay focused on what you believe needs to happen. Always take the high road if someone tries to take you down, and stay the course. Follow up with your people. Assure and *show* them you are trying to do the right thing. Don't let anybody change your ideal. If you know what needs to happen, it's your turn to make it happen. It won't happen overnight, but it can happen."

What story is your center ready to tell? What is the legacy you'll leave?

THE HIGH PERFORMING PSAP

What does it mean to be a high-performing PSAP? Most centers come together when there's a high-profile incident or urgent field situation; but it's what happens during the in-between times that separates the high-performing from the barely-scraping-by. To create consistently high performance, it takes knowing who the right person for the job is. We must hire for the qualities required to usher in this state change. There's no time to teach leaders how to be people driven. They must already possess these qualities.

Once the right person is in the job, they must be supported, elevated, empowered. A People Driven Leader who is hired and then left to wither on the vine will soon grow disenchanted and leave for better opportunities. This support must come in the way of resources (i.e., money) and advocacy. Without the tools to thrive, even the best leader will be unable to make a positive impact.

Even with the right person in place, high performance will still prove elusive if we don't escort the *wrong* people out. The most vocally negative 10% can derail the most well-intentioned change initiative. Set the bar and hold them to a new standard. If they don't conform, use discipline to show the silent majority you mean business.

You can only sustain high performance by keeping sight of the vision, remembering the mission, and telling the story of how yours became an exemplary, People Driven Center.

Despite the examples I've cited of high performance in 9-1-1, very few have achieved it. The truth is, you can't sustain high performance without prioritizing people. Sure, you might have a few months here and there where there weren't too many problems and no one quits, but excellence is what happens when everything *isn't* hunky-dory. How do your people *generally* feel about the place where they work, on a daily basis?

Your high-performance center cannot succeed without doing well in each area outlined in this book. If you find that you're being sucked back down the swirling drain of death, plagued by any of the same old problems, go back through the areas outlined herein, and ask, "How well am I doing?" If the answer is "Not very," then there's an opportunity to attack the problem again. While you don't have to excel in every area, you must address the most severely deficient areas if you hope to stem the immediate challenges your center faces.

A snapshot from a model of personal health and well-being offers a useful metaphor: just as you may continue living for many years with a negative attitude, a few extra pounds and no friends, if your arteries are clogged and you have a heart attack, you will need to take immediate action if you want to continue living. Your communications center is much the same way. With only moderately bad health (several areas are problematic, but none are screaming for attention), you may simply continue doing business as you always have. Once you've identified an area of the organization screaming for your attention, however, you know where to start. As this area begins to improve, you will notice other areas that need your attention.

You will always need to do some level of work to maintain high performance. However, over time, people driven initiatives become self-sustaining. Teams that trust their efforts are valued, who are empowered to innovate, and like the place they work will continue to find additional areas for improvement. A culture of excellence emerges as the way things are done.

It isn't enough to have employees that simply do what they're told. What happens when there's no one around to give orders? An entire organization aligned with what needs to be done, how it's going to get done, and who's going to do it—this type of organization takes self-directed action. And they do it not because they fear what might happen if they don't, but because they are part of the organization's success when they do. This is a People Driven Center.

WHAT IS THE OPPORTUNITY?

Now, more than ever, we are at a crossroad. Since APCO and its Project RETAINS Committee proclaimed an industrywide staffing crisis in 1999, there have been some regional gains; but the landscape is still riddled with similar challenges. More than two decades later, the crisis is still upon us. In fact, it seems to be getting generally worse, except for those who've decided to do something about it.

"In crisis" is an interesting phrase to describe the state of our industry today. In the early 17th century, the term was used to denote the point at which an important change takes place as someone grappled with an illness or a disease. This turning point indicated either recovery or death. Another use of the term means "a time when a difficult or important decision must be made."

We are at that turning point. Recovery *is* possible. But each of us must make the important decision to do something, from wherever we stand today. The status quo is not sustainable and never was. For the thousands across the world who work in the profession—and the millions who depend on the proper functioning of this life-saving service—we must take action, today. We can't wait another 20 years to enact the changes that we know work.

The People Driven Leaders across the country who have turned their centers around are proof that amazing changes are possible. It's not idealism if it's true.

Suggestions for Further Reading

9-1-1 Industry Standards & Research

APCO-ANS-3.102.2-2017: *Core Competencies and Minimum Training Standards for Public Safety Communications Supervisor.* APCO International Communications Center Standards Committee.

APCO-ANS-3.109.1.2014: *Core Competencies and Minimum Training Standards for Public Safety Communications Manager/Director.* APCO International Communications Center Standards Committee.

APCO International. 2018. *Staffing and Retention in Public Safety Answering Points (PSAPs): A Supplemental Study.* George Mason University, Center for Social Science Research.

APCO Project RETAINS. 2005. *Staffing and Retention in Public Safety Communication Centers, Effective Practices Guide and Staffing Workbook.*

APCO Project RETAINS. 2009. *The Compiled Report, Synthesizing Information from the Effective Practices Guide and RETAINS Next Generation.*

APCO/NENA-ANS-1.107.1.2015: *Standard for Establishment of a Quality Assurance and Quality Improvement (QA/QI) Program at Public Safety Answering Points.* APCO International Communications Center Standards Committee.

Change Management

Bridges, W., 2017. *Managing Transitions: Making the Most of Change.* 4th ed. Da Capo.

Dial, C., 2016. *Heretics to Heroes: A Memoir on Modern Leadership.* Bee Cave Publishing.

Heifetz, R., Linsky, M. and Grashow, A., 2009. *The Practice of Adaptive Leadership: Tools and Tactics for Changing Your Organization And The World.* Harvard Business Press.

Lencioni, P., 2005. *Overcoming The Five Dysfunctions Of A Team: A Field Guide For Leaders, Managers And Facilitators.* Jossey-Bass.

Lencioni, P., 2006. *Silos, Politics And Turf Wars: A Leadership Fable About Destroying The Barriers That Turn Colleagues Into Competitors.* 1st ed. John Wiley & Sons.

Senge, P., 1994. *Fifth Discipline Fieldbook: Strategies and Tools for Building a Learning Organization.* Doubleday.

Effective Communication

Patterson, K., 2013. *Crucial Accountability: Tools for Resolving Violated Expectations, Broken Commitments, And Bad Behavior*. 2nd ed. McGraw-Hill.

Patterson, K., Grenny, J., McMillan, R. and Switzler, A., 2011. *Crucial Conversations: Tools for Talking When Stakes Are High*. 2nd ed. McGraw Hill.

Thompson, G. and Jenkins, J., 2013. *Verbal Judo: The Gentle Art of Persuasion*. 2nd ed. William Morrow.

Emotional Intelligence

Bradberry, T. and Greaves, J., 2009. *Emotional Intelligence 2.0*. TalentSmart.

Goleman, D., 1995. *Emotional Intelligence*. New York: Bantam Books.

Harvard Business Review, 2017. *Harvard Business Review Emotional Intelligence Collection*. La Vergne: Harvard Business Review Press.

Employee Engagement

Fowler, S., 2014. *Why Motivating People Doesn't Work...And What Does*. 1st ed. Berrett-Koehler Publishers.

Lencioni, P., 2007. *The Three Signs of A Miserable Job: A Fable For Managers (And Their Employees)*. 1st ed. Wiley.

Marciano, P., 2010. *Carrots and Sticks Don't Work*. New York: McGraw-Hill.

Pink, D., 2009. *Drive: The Surprising Truth About What Motivates Us*. 1st ed. Riverhead Books.

Positive Leadership

Abrashoff, D., 2012. *It's Your Ship: Management Techniques from the Best Damn Ship in the Navy*. New York: Grand Central.

Brown, B., 2015. *Daring Greatly: How the Courage to Be Vulnerable Transforms the Way We Live, Love, Parent and Lead.* Avery.

Gordon, J., 2017. *The Power of Positive Leadership: How and Why Positive Leaders Transform Teams And Organizations And Change The World*. Wiley.

Gordon, J., 2007. *The Energy Bus: 10 Rules to Fuel Your Life, Work, And Team with Positive Energy*. John Wiley & Sons.

Gordon, J., 2008. *The No Complaining Rule: Positive Ways to Deal with Negativity at Work*. John Wiley & Sons.

Gordon, J., 2010. *Soup: A Recipe to Nourish Your Team and Culture*. John Wiley & Sons.

Kouzes, J. and Posner, B., 2012. *The Leadership Challenge: How to Make Extraordinary Things Happen in Organizations*. 5th ed. Wiley.

Sinek, S., 2014. *Leaders Eat Last: Why Some Teams Pull Together and Others Don't*. Penguin.

Sinek, S., 2009. *Start With Why: How Great Leaders Inspire Everyone To Take Action*. Penguin.

Organizational Health

Baker, D., Greenberg, C. and Hemingway, C., 2006. *What Happy Companies Know: How the New Science of Happiness Can Change Your Company for The Better*. 1st ed. Pearson Education.

Keller, S. and Price, C., 2011. *Beyond Performance: How Organizational Health Delivers Ultimate Competitive*. John Wiley & Sons.

Lencioni, P., 2012. *The Advantage: Why Organizational Health Trumps Everything Else in Business*. Jossey-Bass.

Rosen, R. and Berger, L., 1992. *The Healthy Company: Eight Strategies to Develop People, Productivity and Profits*. 1st ed. New York: Putn

ABOUT THE AUTHOR

Adam Timm is a culture change consultant and training session instructor for 9-1-1. He spent over a decade as a 9-1-1 dispatcher for the Los Angeles Police Department, where he pioneered a stress resilience program that contributed to a 45% decrease in sick time usage. After leaving the LAPD, Adam started his company *The Healthy Dispatcher* to bring tools for change to this challenging profession.

He is a board-certified stress management consultant and the author of three books, including the #1 bestseller, "Stress Is Optional! How to Kick the Habit," and the popular, "Dispatcher Stress: 50 Lessons on Beating the Burnout." Adam's articles on Dispatcher Wellness and Effective PSAP Leadership have been read by tens of thousands.

HOW TO WORK WITH US

If you'd like assistance with implementing any of the strategies you read about here, we'd love to talk with you. In addition to Adam, The Healthy Dispatcher team is comprised of accomplished 9-1-1 managers and directors from exemplary 9-1-1 communications centers across the country. To learn more about working with us to bring positive change to your center, please visit us on our website:

www.thehealthydispatcher.com

or email Adam directly at:
adam@thehealthydispatcher.com

The services The Healthy Dispatcher provides:

- 360-degree Culture Assessment
- Leadership Assessment/Evaluation
- Review/Revision of SOPs, Training Program, QA Program
- Mission, Vision, Values Statement Development
- Paneled Interviews & Leadership Candidate Review
- Leadership Team Building
- Communication & Conflict Resolution Training
- Stress Resilience Training
- Emotional Intelligence Training
- Customized programs to fit your center's specific needs

Made in United States
Orlando, FL
23 June 2023